Business, Government and Economics

John Pratten & Nigel Proctor

TUDOR

© J. Pratten & N. Proctor 1999

First published in Great Britain by Tudor Business Publishing Limited.

A CIP catalogue for this book is available from the British Library

ISBN 1 872807 58 5

The right of John Pratten and Nigel Proctor to be identified as the authors
of this work has been asserted by them in accordance with the
Copyright, Designs and Patents Act 1988.

Typeset by Bitter & Twisted, N. Wales

Printed and Bound in Great Britain by
Athenaeum Press Ltd, Newcastle upon Tyne

To Lesley, Anthony and Felicity,
Amanda, Zoë and Gregory

introduction

The authors believe that too frequently business studies and economics, the study of the economy in which businesses exist, are treated in isolation thus providing an incomplete picture. The influence of government is also largely ignored and left to those who study politics or a related political course. This text considers all of the topic areas that influence or interact with the functioning of a business in a straightforward and accessible manner. It has been specifically designed to provide a comprehensive grounding in the areas of business studies, economics and government, consequently it is ideally suited to those students who are studying for professional examinations and require a basic knowledge of all these subject areas. More specifically the text has been aimed at undergraduates who are studying business or business related subjects for the first time.

The text makes the maximum use of visual materials, current data and worked examples. At the end of each chapter the reader is provided with the opportunity to reflect upon the work covered in the chapter. The questions provided are intended to stimulate interest and encourage debate but, as is typical for this subject area, they have many possible answers.

As experienced examiners and lecturers we are concerned that all too frequently students have an incomplete basic knowledge of business, economics and government. We are convinced that this text will fill the gap.

John Pratten
Nigel Proctor

contents

one

The Economic Problem and Some Solutions   1

two

The Development and Growth of Industry   38

three

The Economic Institutions   59

four

The Governmental Framework   73

five

The Decision Makers   84

six

Unemployment, Inflation and Economic Growth   98

seven

International Trade   126

eight

The Problems of Government Economic Policy   151

chapter one

The Economic Problem and Some Solutions

The basic economic problems and decisions that give rise to economics as a discipline

1.1 Scarcity

1.2 Choice

1.3 The Price Mechanism and the Market

1.4 Costs and Revenue

1.5 The Circular Flow of Income

1.6 The Economic System

This section should enable students to:

■ explain the nature of the economic problem

■ understand the workings of the market and the determination of price

■ understand the significance of the circular flow of income

■ recognise the different solutions to the economic problem

1.1 Scarcity

Wants and Needs

People all over the world have different wants and needs. All countries have basic needs for items such as food and water. In Less Developed Countries (LDCs) these basic needs are often in very short supply. In the more advanced countries the basic needs are usually ample and are replaced with a desire for other things. These items are not really necessary for survival: they are what people want rather than what they need.

As the basic needs are satisfied people turn their attention to new items that they think they need. People are never satisfied with what they have and this is true of the rich as well as the poor. If you rent a house you want to buy your own. If you own your own house you want a bigger one and then one with bigger grounds and a double garage.

It is possible for everyone to produce a list of what they want. If these wants were satisfied it would be a simple task to produce another list and then another. This happens because even when the requirement is just food and shelter there is an enormous difference between a basic need and what is wanted. Stale bread is food but so is caviar; a wooden hut is shelter but so is Buckingham Palace. A family of six will need a larger house than a single person; could they therefore say that a four-bedroom detached house is a basic need? It is clearly difficult to show the difference between people's wants and needs.

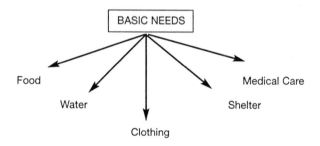

Figure 1.1 People's Basic Needs

The confusion between what human beings need and what they think they want creates a desire for more and more. This desire can be described as ambition, trying to improve one's lifestyle, or greed.

However it is described, the presence of this desire in people produces a never-ending demand for goods and services. This is increased by the fact that goods are used up or wear out and need replacing, or are replaced by better versions. The result is that the human race possesses an unlimited demand for goods and services.

If everyone's wants and needs are to be satisfied a constant supply of goods and services must be produced. This is only possible if there are enough resources, an unlimited supply of resources, to produce everything that is demanded. Unlimited demand should be matched by unlimited supply. The problem is that the resources needed for production, raw materials, workers, machinery and buildings, are limited in supply.

Factors of Production

The resources, known as the factors of production, are the factors land, labour, capital and enterprise. The factor land is used to describe all the raw materials beneath the ground and in the seas and rivers, as well as on the surface of the land and grown on the earth's surface. Labour is human effort, work performed by the workforce. The workforce includes all of those willing and able to work. Capital is the machinery, factories and buildings used to help and increase output. Enterprise is the organising factor, the person who makes the decisions and takes the risks, the 'boss'.

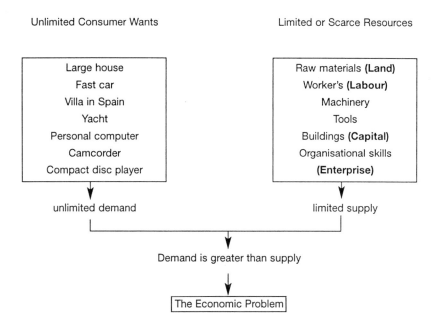

Figure 1.2 The Economic Problem

All these factors are limited in supply. We do not possess an unlimited supply of labour or oil or land on which to build. If the factors of production are limited or scarce then the supply of goods and services will be limited and the unlimited demand cannot be satisfied. This creates a problem, the economic problem: how can people's unlimited demands be satisfied?

If limitation or scarcity of resources means that not all demand can be satisfied then choices have to be made. The role of economic decision making becomes important. It must be decided how best to satisfy as many of the wants and needs as possible. The whole reason for the existence of economics is to solve this economic problem.

1.2 Choice

What to Produce?

The economic problem is faced by every country and community. Everywhere resources are limited or scarce, and demand is unlimited, but in some countries the problem is more obvious than in others. A commodity that is scarce in one county or in another community is not necessarily scarce elsewhere.

If resources are scarce and all the people's wants and needs cannot be satisfied, what is needed is organisation, a way of producing as much as possible with the resources available to satisfy as many of the wants and needs as possible. This form of organisation is called an economy.

Different economies around the world exist because there are many different solutions to the economic problem. Economic decisions are made by different groups or in different ways and this produces entirely different types of economic system (Chapter 1.6).

If it is impossible to produce everything that people want and need then the first economic decision to be made is what to produce. The government can decide what to produce. Alternatively the consumers can make decisions through their demand for goods and services.

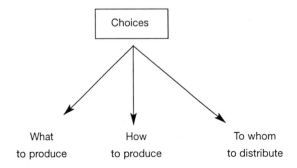

Figure 1.3 The Economic Problem

A third solution is to use a combination of the two methods already described. The method used to decide what to produce is a major factor in determining the type of economy that exists. Every economy tends to solve the problem in a difference way.

Opportunity Cost

Whatever the method used to decide what to produce, a choice has to be made and that choice involves a cost. For every item (good) or service produced something has to be given up, a sacrifice has to be made. This cost is explained in economics as the opportunity cost.

The opportunity cost of any item is the next best alternative that has to be given up. If an individual has five hours of spare time and decides to watch the television rather than finish an assignment the opportunity cost of watching the television is the assignment that has not been finished. Opportunity cost is a part of everyone's life. All economic goods have an opportunity cost. Every day everyone makes choices in their life: what to buy, what to eat and how to spend their time. All of these involve opportunity costs.

Firms have to make the choice of what to produce and it is very important for them. If they use their raw materials, labour and capital to build offices they cannot build houses with the same resources; this is the opportunity cost. Governments have to make decisions about the way in which they spend their money. Should it be on education, health, defence, reducing the tax rate or increasing unemployment benefits? If they have £20 billion the opportunity cost of spending £10 billion on defence is the £10 billion they could have spent on health.

One of the biggest decisions that has to be made is whether an economy should produce consumer goods and services or capital goods. Capital goods, such as factories and machines, increase output in the future giving everybody more to enjoy. The cost, the opportunity cost, of increasing output in the future is a decrease in the output of consumer goods and services now. Consumer goods and capital goods cannot both be produced using the same resources; a choice has to be made.

Figure 1.4 shows how the concept of opportunity cost actually works. If a country has a set amount of the factors of production then it can either produce all consumer goods (point A) or it can produce all capital goods (point B). It cannot produce at point A and at point B. Between points A and B are a number of different combinations of consumer goods and capital goods that can be produced with a set amount of the factors of production. These combinations are shown by the line joining points A and B together, the production possibility frontier.

If this country produces at point F they can produce 'OD' units of consumer goods and 'OE' units of capital goods. If they then decide to move to point G increasing consumer good output and decreasing capital good output an opportunity cost is involved. The opportunity costs of increasing consumer goods by 'DJ' units is 'HE' units of capital that are lost.

In some communities the decision between consumer and capital goods is extremely serious. If resources are used to produce capital goods the opportunity cost is those people who will not have enough food to eat. If capital goods are not produced the opportunity cost of producing food now is those people who will die in the future due to a lack of food as the population increases.

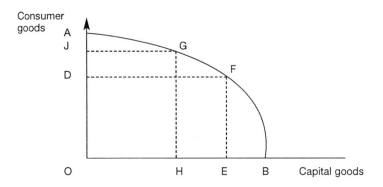

Figure 1.4 Opportunity Cost

How to Produce

Once the decision of what to produce has been made the next step is to decide how to produce. This will be decided by the type of produce or service to be produced, the amount of labour and capital available.

Production can be capital intensive, using more machinery than labour, or labour intensive, using more labour than capital. If the community has a large supply of labour and very little capital, or a poor level of technology, then a labour-intensive method would make more sense. However, if the level of technology in the country was very advanced with a small highly skilled population, a capital intensive method would be more appropriate.

In some cases the choice of production method is determined by the good or service itself. Delivery of letters or cutting people's hair cannot be done by using capital-intensive methods. Handmade furniture needs skilled craftsmen, not machines. If only small quantities of a good are required capital intensive methods would again not be suitable.

The decision 'how to produce' is not influenced by the type of economy but by other factors. The production method used does not determine, or influence, the type of economy.

Distribution

The final decision that has to be made to overcome the economic problem is how to distribute the goods and services produced. All the goods and services produced can be shared out according to tradition: the elder comes first, the worker comes first, the religious leader takes precedence, and so on.

A second solution would be for everything to be shared out according to people's ability to pay. Those that can afford the goods and services can have them, those that cannot go without.

A third solution would be for everyone to have an equal share of everything produced. This would need the state to own the factors of production and individuals to have total equality.

The final alternative is that some goods such as health and education should be shared equally, and other goods, consumer durables, according to people's ability to pay.

Review Terms

Command economy; market economy; mixed economy; consumer sovereignty; public sector; private sector; opportunity cost; consumer goods; capital goods; production possibility frontier; capital intensive; labour intensive.

1.3   The Price Mechanism and the Market

Demand

Individuals have different wants and needs and if they are to be satisfied a variety of goods and services must be produced. The problem is which goods and services? How do the producers know which items to provide? What is required is a method of giving the producers the information they need, what to produce, how many and at what price.

There are people who want goods but are unable to purchase them. This is of no use to a producer. There are also those people who are able to purchase a good or service but have no desire to do so. They are also of no use to a producer of goods and services.

What a producer needs is people who wish to buy and have the money to buy the good, or service. This is known as effective demand

■ Effective demand exists when people are willing and able to purchase a good or service.

If people do not have the ability to purchase, as well as the willingness, then their wants and needs are little more than a dream and of no practical use to producers. It is their desire as well as their ability that provides the producer with the right information to produce the goods and services that people want and can afford to buy.

People demanding goods and services act as a sophisticated information system; they can register what type of goods and services they require, in what quantities and at what prices. If any of these preferences change then they alter their demand to change the signals that are being given.

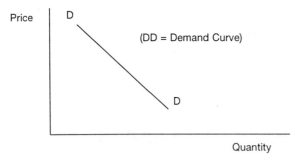

Figure 1.5 The Demand Curve

The demand that a person has for a particular good or service can be represented graphically. If a person demands a set quantity of good, then, if the price of that good increases, they will buy less. The opposite is also true that if the price of that good decreases they will buy more. This shows a relationship between price and quantity demanded for a particular good. Figure 1.5 shows the relationship between price and quantity and this is an individual demand curve.

■ A demand curve shows the quantity of a good and service demanded by an individual at each and every price during a specified time period.

The convention is that price is plotted on the vertical axis and quantity along the horizontal axis. The individual curve usually slopes down from left to right. Price and quantity are said to be inversely related; as price increases the quantity demanded decreases and vice versa.

If individual demand curves are aggregated for the same good or service they form a market demand curve. The market demand curve is also usually downward sloping from left to right, even though some individuals may have different shaped demand curves. Thus the market demand curve looks exactly like the individual demand curve shown in figure 1.5.

There are exceptions to this rule. In special circumstances the demand curve can be horizontal, vertical or sloping up from left to right. The backward sloping demand curve, known as the perverse demand curve, occurs in special situations where the quantity demanded increases as price increases. This can be found with 'snob value' goods such as jewellery, furs and cars such as Rolls Royce. The more expensive they are the more they are demanded because they are a statement of wealth. The other situation is rising share prices. As share prices go up the more they are demanded because purchasers believe that this company must be doing well.

Changes in Quantity Demanded

The normal shaped demand curve can produce a number of different situations. It is possible to move along the demand curve or the whole demand curve is caused by a change in price. This is known as a change in the quantity demanded. Figure 1.6 shows the effect of the price changing from Po to P1; this creates a change in the quantity demanded, decreasing from Qo to Q1. The movement along the demand curve is from point 'a' to point 'b'; this can only happen when the price of the good or service changes. This creates the general rule that 'changes' in the price of a good create a change in the quantity demanded, which is a movement along the demand curve.

The movement along the curve from point 'a' to point 'b' creates a decrease in the quantity demanded this is known as a contraction in demand. A movement from point 'b' to point 'a' would create an increase in the quantity demanded, described as an extension in demand or an expansion of demand.

Changes in Demand

When the whole demand curve moves it means that at each and every price people are demanding more or less of the good in question; this must be due to influences other than price. A major factor that influences demand is income. If an individual's income increases then he or she can afford more goods and services, assuming that the prices of these goods and services remain unchanged. Thus at each and every

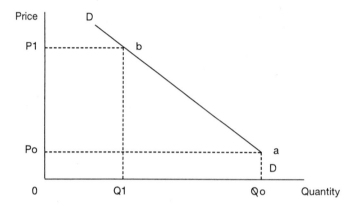

Figure 1.6 Extension and Contraction of Demand

price the quantity demanded would increase. This would be an increase in demand shown by a movement of the whole curve to the right, as in figure 1.7.

If income were to decrease then an individual would decrease his or her demand for a good or service at each and every price. This in turn would move the whole curve to the left, as in figure 1.7.

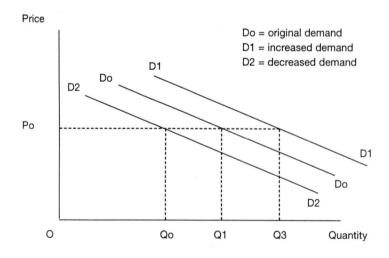

Figure 1.7 Changes in Demand

A movement of the whole curve to the right is an increase in demand. A movement of the whole curve to the left is a decrease in demand.

Another factor that influences demand is change in taste and fashion. When goods become fashionable people wish to buy more. The demand for these good increases and the curve moves to the right.

The season or climate can increase or decrease demand. In the summer the demand for suncream increases, although the price is the same throughout the year. At the same time the demand for umbrellas and wellingtons decreases but, once again, not because of a change in price.

A situation that links together figure 1.6 and figure 1.7 is the change in price of a substitute. Substitutes are goods that are an acceptable replacement for one another. For example, chicken and beef are substitutes for each other as are Ford and Rover cars.

If the price of holidays abroad increased the quantity demanded would decrease. This is shown in figure 1.6 by a movement from point 'a' to point 'b'. The people that stop buying holidays abroad (quantity Qo to Q1) would then buy the substitute holidays in the UK. The demand for UK holidays would therefore increase and the whole curve would move to the right, as in figure 1.7. Similarly if the price of butter decreased then more people would buy butter and the demand for margarine would decrease, the curve moving to the left. The change in the price of one good creates a transfer of demand for another product, an acceptable substitute. This is known as the income and substitution effect.

Some goods are complementary, for example cars and petrol. Cars will not run without petrol and petrol itself has very few uses except to drive a car. If the price of cars were to increase the quantity demanded would decrease. If less cars were purchased then the demand for petrol would decrease and the demand curve would move to the left.

Advertising is a deliberate attempt by producers to move the demand curve to the right. Advertisers try to influence people by convincing them of the value and special qualities of their good, hoping they will buy more. Bad publicity has the opposite effect, moving the demand curve to the left. A good example is the press coverage of 'mad cow disease' which decreased the demand for beef.

Expectations of price change create a change in demand. If it known that the price of coffee is to rise next month because of a shortage of coffee beans then people will go out and buy more coffee now before the shortage occurs. This will increase demand even though it is only temporary.

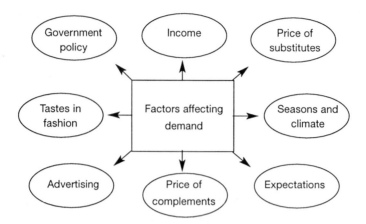

Figure 1.8 Factors Affecting Demand

Finally, government policy can change demand. If the government decided to ban smoking for everyone under 25 the demand for cigarettes would decrease. The policy that all new cars must be fitted with catalytic converters has increased the demand for them. The effect can also be indirect: when the government decreased the tax on new cars this increased the quantity purchased. The indirect effect was to increase the demand for petrol, a complimentary good.

Supply

Demand is of little use unless someone is prepared to produce the goods and services that people are willing and able to buy. The fact that people are prepared to produce goods and services creates a supply.

■ Supply exists when producers are willing and able to offer goods and services for sale.

As with demand it is important that producers are willing and able to supply. Without both elements supply will not exist. The supply of goods and services provided by any one individual, or single firm, can be represented graphically. A firm offers goods and services for sale because it is believed that it will make a profit from the transaction. The higher the price paid for an item the more profit is made and the more items firms are willing to supply. This produces the opposite relationship to that of demand: as the price increases the quantity offered for sale by the producers also increases.

Once again the convention is that quantity is plotted on the horizontal axis and the price on the vertical axis. Therefore the supply curve is upward sloping from left to right.

■ A supply curve shows the quantity of a good or service offered for sale at each and every price during a specified period of time.

In this case price and quantity are positvely related; as price increases so does the quantity supplied.

If individual supply curves are added together a market supply curve can be produced. This is the same shape as the individual supply curve, figure 1.9, with a few exceptions. The major difference is that the quantities along the horizontal axis are much greater.

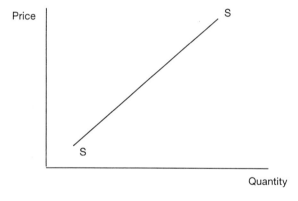

Figure 1.9 The Supply Curve

Changes in the Quantity Supplied

When price changes it causes a movement along the supply curve, as with demand in figure 1.6. This is known as a change in the quantity supplied. Figure 1.10 shows the effect of price moving from Po and P1, which creates a change in the quantity supplied, increasing from Qo to Q1. The movement along the supply curve is from point 'e' to point 'f', which can only happen when the price of the good or service changes. This creates a general rule for supply.

■ Changes in the price of a good or service create a change in the quantity supplied, which is a movement along the supply curve.

Movement from point 'e' to point 'f' is an extension or expansion of supply (Qo to Q1). A decrease in price from P1 to Po would create movement along the supply curve from point 'f' to point 'e' and this would be a contraction of supply (Q1 to Qo).

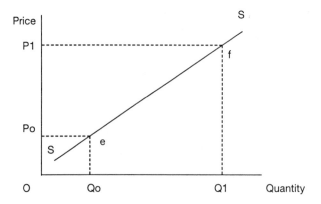

Figure 1.10 Changes in the Quanitity Supplied

Changes in Supply

Whilst changes in price create a movement along the supply curve there are factors that move the whole supply curve, either to the left (a decrease in supply) or to the right (an increase in supply). The supply curve is heavily influenced by a firm's ability to produce the item concerned and the costs of production. Thus changes in either of these will move the whole supply curve.

The cost of labour (wages) is possibly the biggest cost faced by any producer. If wages increase, the costs of production increase, which moves the whole supply curve to the left (an upward shift), which shows a decrease in supply. The same would happen if the cost of raw materials and equipment also increased. If any of the costs of production decreased, whilst the rest remained the same, then the whole curve would move to the right, producing an increase in supply at the set price.

Changes in technology, such as new inventions or new methods of production, usually allow producers to make an item more cheaply or at a faster speed. The result is to increase the supply of the good at the present price, moving the curve to the right.

The weather has a special influence on the supply of agricultural products. Good weather usually means an increased supply of goods, because of the right growing conditions, whereas poor weather often affects the growing season and so decreases the supply.

Natural disasters, such as earthquakes, floods and fires, all have an adverse effect on the supply of goods and usually move the curve to the left, due to a decreased supply.

Taxes on production such as VAT (value added tax) or government subsidies either decrease or increase the costs of production and in turn affect the supply of a product. VAT is added to the cost of production and so increases the costs of production. This decreases supply, moving the the curve to the left. A government subsidy is used to help output by decreasing the cost of production. If the cost of production decreases then output will increase, moving the curve to the right.

Strikes and inefficient management will decrease output, or make the firm less productive which will increase the cost of production. The result in both of these cases is that the supply curve will move to the left, a decrease in supply.

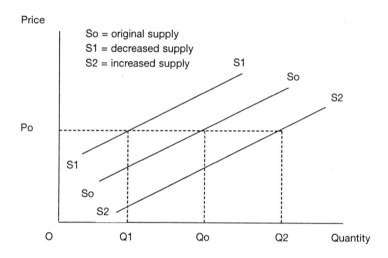

Figure 1.11 Changes in Supply

The Market

Demand for a product without supply or the supply of a product without demand produces nothing. Both elements need to exist at the same time. It is only when demand and supply exist for the same product that a market is formed.

■ A market exists whenever buyers and sellers come into contact with each other.

This can be physical contact, over the telephone, via a fax or by using the pages of a local newspaper, where sellers advertise their goods and buyers scan the pages to find the product that they wish to buy.

Buyers create a demand, and sellers create a supply. A market exists when demand and supply interact. This interaction creates an equlibrium which in turn creates a market price. Figure 1.12 shows a demand and a supply for Christmas cards. If we assume that the demand and supply does not change (ceteris paribus - all other things remain equal) then the market will find its own equilibrium and a market price will be determined.

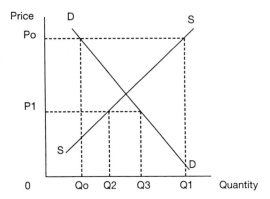

Figure 1.12 Market Disequilibrium

Using figure 1.12, if the Christmas cards are offered for sale at a price Po then demand will equal quantity Qo and supply will equal Q1. Supply will be greater than demand and the producers will have spare unsold cards on their hands, an excess supply. In this situation the supplier will have to decrease the price of the cards in order to encourage people to buy them. Thus the price will drop from Po. If the price was to be set at P1 then demand, at quantity Q3, would be greater than supply, at quantity Q2, and there would be a shortage of cards. The supplier in this case would increase the price, selling them to the highest bidder. If price is at P1, it will increase.

The point at which price neither increases or decreases is where demand equals supply. At this point all of the cards being offered for sale are being purchased. The market is said to be in equilibrium, balanced until either demand or supply changes. Figure 1.13 shows the market equilibrium. Equilibrium will exist as long as neither demand nor supply changes.

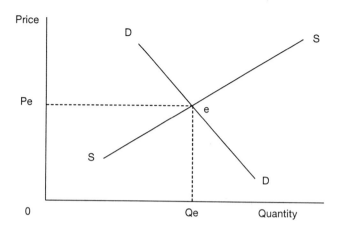

Figure 1.13 Market Equilibrium

At this point the signals given by the consumers have been correctly received by the producers and the correct quantity of resources has been allocated to the production of the good or service. The result is that the right quantity has been produced at the right price.

If demand were to increase (see figure 1.14) due to an increase in consumers' income, possibly due to a reduction in the income tax rate, more goods would be demanded. This would disturb the equilibrium situation and the resources would need to be allocated because of the new messages being given out.

If figure 1.14 represents the market for a product then equilibrium exists when the price is Po and the quantity demanded and supplied equals Qo at point 'a'. Everything in the market is balanced. If demand increases to D1D1, as previously described, then the equilibrium is disturbed. The quantity demanded is now 0Q2, and the quantity supplied equals 0Qo. This creates a new set of messages for the market:

- demand is greater than supply;

- more resources are needed to produce this good.

The producers are not prepared to produce 0Q2 units at Po. If they supply more they want a higher price. Therefore, the price will increase and the quantity supplied will also increase. The increase in price attracts new resources and enables more to be produced. Gradually the market will produce more at a higher price until demand equals supply at point 'b'. At this point the quantity demanded equals 0Q1 and the quantitiy supplied also equals 0Q1. Equilibrium is restored and the market has successfully attracted new resources, rationing the goods available to the highest bidders, at price P1.

If new technology is introduced which decreases the cost of production, then the supply curve moves to the right, and there is an increase in supply . In this situation supply is greater than demand, the price drops as the excess supply is sold and resources are diverted to more profitable uses. Eventually a new equilibrium is achieved at a lower price but at an increased quantity.

It is the role of the market to transmist signals between consumers and producers in order to allocate resources according to need. The price signals the value of output and as price increases more resources are directed to the production of that good. As price decreases the resources are taken away and used for more profitable production. The signals of demand, supply and price should eventually achieve an equilibrium where all of the resources are allocated efficiently.

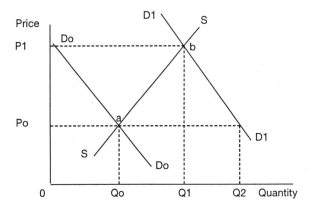

Figure 1.14 Changing Market Equilibrium

In the real world, because things are constantly changing, markets are rarely in equilibrium. They are usually trying to reach an equilibrium. Also many markets are not free to work properly; they are influenced or restricted by forces such as the government or trade unions. This does not mean that the market is inefficient but that it is often unable to work in the way that it should.

Review Terms

Effective demand; individual demand; market demand; perverse demand; extension/contraction of demand; substitutes; complements; income and substitution effect; expectations; market supply; extension/contraction of supply; excess supply; market equilibrium; market price.

1.4   Costs and Revenues

Revenue

Revenue is the amount of money that a business receives for the sale of goods and services. Total revenue is the price of each item sold multiplied by the quantity sold, or the total value of sales.

■   Total revenue = Price x Quantity

Costs

The total cost of running a business is split into two parts. Fixed costs are those costs which do not change, no matter how much is produced. They are constant, and include such items as rent, rates and insurance. Variable costs are those costs which change according to how much is produced. They are zero when nothing is made, but gradually increase as the quantity produced increases. They include wages, the purchase of raw materials and the cost of power.

■   Total costs = Fixed costs + Variable costs

Profit

All firms aim to make a profit. Profit is the difference between the revenue collected for selling goods and services and the costs of making those goods and services.

■   Total profit = Total revenue - Total cost

Total profit forms only part of the information that firms need to know to ensure maximum profits. It may be helpful to know the profit per unit, and whether total profit could be increased by producing a greater or smaller quantity of the product.

Profit Per Unit

Profit per unit is especially important if a firm is producing serveral different items, or have just begun to sell a new product. To calculate profit per unit, it is necessary to find the cost and the revenue per unit.

Quantity Produced £	Fixed Cost £	Variable Cost £	Total Cost £
0	100	0	100
1	100	20	120
2	100	38	138
3	100	50	150
4	100	60	160
5	100	65	165
6	100	74	174

Figure 1.15 Calculations to Find Profit per Unit

Average cost = $\dfrac{\text{Total cost}}{\text{Quantity}}$

Average revenue = $\dfrac{\text{Total revenue}}{\text{Quantity}}$

If total revenue minus total costs gives total profit then:

Profit per unit = Average revenue - Average cost

This can be all put together in on a chart (figure 1.16) which shows that the maximum level of proift would be £90, with a production of three units. However, the maximum profit per unit is £31 with a production of two units, but this would give a total profit of only £62. This gives two conflicting pieces of information, and the decision on how much to produce will depend on the aims of the firm.

Quantity	Price (£)	Total Revenue (£)	Total Cost (£)	Total Profit (£)	Average Revenue (£)	Average Cost (£)	Profit per Unit
0	150	0	100	-100	-	-	-
1	120	120	120	0	120	120	0
2	100	200	138	62	100	69	31
3	80	240	150	90	80	50	30
4	60	240	160	80	60	40	20
5	40	200	165	35	40	33	7
6	20	120	174	-54	20	29	-9

Table 1.16 Table Showing Profit Per Unit

If the quantities were in thousands, rather than single units, the maximum profit is unlikely to be exactly £3,000, but somewhere around that figure. If this could be calculated, then the firm would have even more detailed information on which to base its decisions.

Maximum Profit

The method to find maximum profit involves marginal costs and marginal revenues. Marginal cost is the extra cost of producing one more unit. If it costs £120 to produce one unit and £138 to produce two units, then the cost involved in increasing production from one unit to two is £18. This is the marginal cost. Marginal revenue is the extra revenue received from the sale of one extra unit. If the total revenue from selling one unit is £120, but the sale of two units would give a total revenue of £200, then the extra revenue resulting from the sale of the extra unit is £80. This is the marginal revenue.

It is possible to calculate the marginal costs and marginal revenues and to plot a graph of them. Each marginal cost and marginal revenue represents the difference between the totals. For example, between sales of one and two the marginal revenue is £80. This is not at a sale of one or two, but in between, so the graph would be plotted between one and two.

Quantity Revenue	Total Revenue £	Marginal Revenue £	Total Cost £	Marginal Cost £
0	0		100	
		120		20
1	120		120	
		80		18
2	200		138	
		40		12
3	240		150	
		0		10
4	240		160	
		-40		5
5	200		165	
		-80		9
6	120		174	

Figure 1.17 Marginal Revenues and Marginal Costs

If the marginal revenue received from selling a unit is greater than the marginal cost involved in making it, then a profit is being made in the production of that unit. When the marginal cost is greater than the marginal revenue, then a loss is being made in the production of that unit.

Thus, to maximise profits a firm should continue production up to the point where marginal revenue ceases to be greater than marginal costs.

Break-Even Analysis

It is possible to use some of the information relating to cost and revenue in order to calculate the minimum number of sales that a firm needs to make before it enters into profit. Looking at figure 1.18, it is clear that, at an output of one unit, total cost is the same as total revenue, so there is neither profit nor loss.

At an output of two units, revenue is greater than cost, so a profit is being made. This is best expressed diagrammatically, as in figure 1.19. Quantity is plotted on the horizontal axis and cost/revenue on the vertical axis.

Quantity £	Fixed Costs £	Variable Costs £	Total Costs £	Total Revenue £
0	100	0	100	0
1	100	20	120	120
2	100	38	138	200
3	100	50	150	240
4	100	60	160	240
5	100	65	165	200
6	100	74	174	120

Figure 1.18 Figures Necessary for the Calculation of Minimum Sales Required

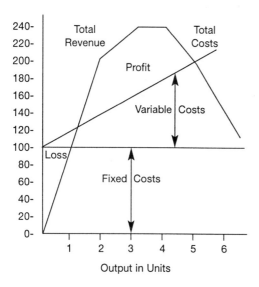

Figure 1.19 Diagram to Show the Analysis of Break-even Point

The fixed cost curve is drawn, and then the variable cost curve plotted above it. This will also be the total cost curve. Then the total revenue curve is added. Where the total revenue curve meets the total cost curve, the break-even point has been reached.

As long as total revenue is above total costs, a profit is being made.

Review Terms

Revenue; total revenue; fixed costs; variable costs; total costs; profit; profit per unit; average costs; average revenue; maximum profit; marginal costs; marginal revenue; break-even point.

1.5   Circular Flow of Income

The Basic Economic Problem

The function of any economy is to solve the basic economic problem.   Scarce resources, created by a shortage of the factors of production, labour, land, capital and enterprise, and people's unlimited demand for goods and services, creates this problem. It is impossible to produce everything that people want and need and so choices have to be made. The first decision is what to produce, and the second is how to produce the goods and services that we need. Finally, to whom to distribute concerns how we share out those goods and services that have been produced. All economies face these problems but it is the way in which they are solved that determines what an economy is like.

Two Sector Economy

In order to appreciate how an economy solves the problem of scarcity it is important to understand how it works. Tracing a path of money around an economy helps to explain how it works.

Assume a simple two sector economy of firms and households with no government and no international trade. This is a closed economy. If we start at the production stage, the manufacturing of goods and the production of services, all of the factors of production are required. In order to take part in the production process all of these factors require payments, or rewards. Labour needs wages, land receives rent, capital receives interest and enterprise gains the reward of profit. Therefore, production creates income (Y) in the form of wages, rent, interest and profit (WRIP). This money income is passed on to the owners of the factors of production, the households (individuals).

The households, when they receive their income, have two choices of what to do with it. They can save it, savings (S), or use it to buy goods and services, which is consumption (C). Consumption is buying goods and services to satisfy wants and needs and saving is that income which is not spent on consumer goods and services but placed in a bank or building society, or some other financial institution.   The amount that is saved or used for consumption is determined by many factors such as the amount of income, trends and fashions and the rate of interest (the cost of borrowing money).

Buying consumer goods and services, consumption, creates effective demand in the market. People have the ability to purchase and wish to do so. This is registered by the producers as a demand for their product and so they respond by producing what is demanded.

Some savings may be put in a box or under the bed: this is real savings. The fact that individuals put their savings into financial institutions provides a fund of money for producers to borrow. The financial institutions then lend the money that they have collected, in the form of savings, to firms who wish to improve or purchase new capital. The purchase of capital is investment, which creates a demand for capital goods.

Thus demand is created by consumption and investment which produces a total demand for all of the goods and services produced in the economy, both capital and consumer goods. The level of total demand determines production and completes the circular flow. The total demand created is expressed as a single monetary figure, the aggregate monetary demand (AMD). The total is arrived at by adding together the monetary demand for all the goods and services that exist (price x quantity x all the goods and services). Figure 1.20 shows the simple two sector economy.

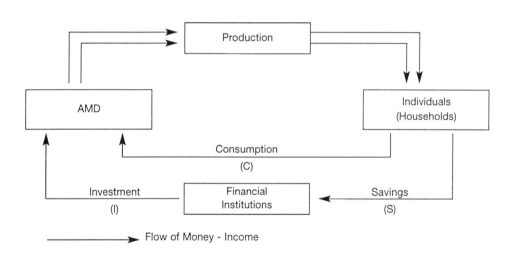

Figure 1.20 The Simple Two Sector Economy

If money flows around this economy from stage to stage then the level of AMD determines the level of output which in turn determines the level of income. Therefore AMD is equivalent to output which is equivalent to income.

AMD = Output = Income

At the household stage income can be split into consumption (C) and savings (S). In a shorthand style this can be written as

$$Y = C + S$$

AMD, which is equivalent to income (Y), is made up of a demand for consumer goods and services (C) plus a demand for capital goods, investment (I). This can also be written in shorthand style.

$$Y = C + I$$

If the two equations above are compared:

$$Y = C + S \text{ and } Y = C + I$$

then:
$$C + S = C + I$$

and therefore
$$S = I.$$

This identity produces what is know as an equilibrium condition. When the level of savings equals the level of investment the circular flow will be perfectly balanced and will not change. This equilibrium condition only applies to the two sector economy.

Injections and Withdrawals

Savings put under the bed or into a box can be lost to the circular flow, but so can savings put into financial institutions. There is no reason why the financial institutions should lend out all of the money that is saved with them, except that they wish to make a profit. If firms do not wish to borrow money to invest then real savings will leave the circular flow and not return until needed This is a leakage, or withdrawal, from the circular flow. The term leakage implies an accidental removal but saving is a conscious effort, therefore the preferred term is 'withdrawal'.

Investment is not a withdrawal. It is money put into the circular flow. Financial institutions have the ability to create money, and can actually lend more money than they have available through savings. Investment is an extra amount of money put into the circular flow which increases the size of the economy. It is called an injection. The people investing and those saving are usually different, with different motives.

The aim of those investing is to make money that they do not currently have to purchase capital goods. The aim of those saving is to put aside an amount of money for the future, or for a special reason. To simplify the situation, in the following discussion it is assumed that all borrowing is for investment.

If savings is a withdrawal (S=W) from the circular flow and investment is an injection (I=J) into the circular flow, the equilibrium condition can now be generalised to withdrawals equal injections (W=J). The equilibrium condition for all of the circular flow models is :

Withdrawals (W) = Injections (J).

The Three Sector Economy

The three sector model includes firms, households and a government sector. It is still a closed economy with no international trade. Production still creates income, but the difference in this model is that the government takes its share of the factor incomes in the form of direct taxation (T). Income is now divided into consumption, savings and taxation. The income before taxation is gross income and what is left after taxation is net income. Net income, disposable income, is then split between consumption and savings.

At the demand stage (AMD), there is a demand for consumer goods (C) and capital goods (I), plus a demand by the government for goods and services. Government expenditure (G) is used to provide merit goods and public goods, purchase capital for state-run industries or consumable items such as paper for schools and medical supplies for hospitals.

The money that the government has to spend comes either from tax revenues or from borrowing (the public sector borrowing requirement - PSBR). Government expenditure forms part of the AMD which determines production. Aggregate monetary demand is now consumption plus investment plus government expenditure.

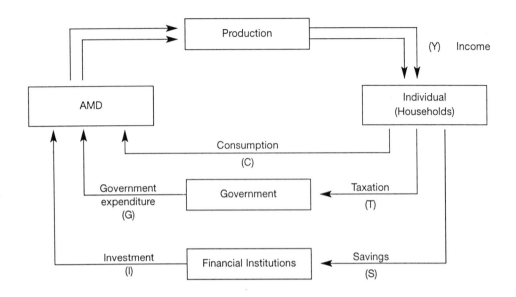

Figure 1.21 Three Sector Circular Flow

The Open Economy

The simplfied open model includes households, firms, the government and international trade. Production still creates income for the owners of the factors of production, but this income is now split into four parts. Firstly the income is taxed, producing disposable income, and then the remainder is either saved, used for consumption of home-produced goods or used to purchase foreign goods and services, imports (M)

Aggregate monetary demand is still consumption plus investment plus government expenditure, but also includes the demand by households overseas for goods and services produced in the home economy, exports (X). Export demand is therefore part of AMD.

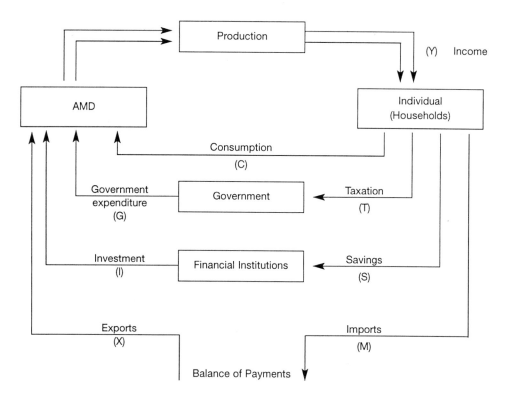

Figure 1.22 The Open Model

Injections and Withdrawals

In the two sector model savings is a withdrawal and investment an injection. The equilibrium condition is that injections should equal withdrawls.

Government expenditure is also an injection because it is money put into the economy by the government. Although the money spent by the government is often taken from taxation, it can be money borrowed. Governments regularly spend more than they collect in tax. Equally, governments may wish to tax but not to spend the resulting money; this would be a withdrawal. There is no reason why government tax and expenditure should be equal. Therefore, expenditure is an injection and taxation is a withdrawal.

Money spent on imports is clearly a withdrawal. It is leaving the circular flow and entering the economy of another country. Exports are very clearly injections. This is money from other economies being injected into our circular flow creating a demand for home-produced goods and services. The level of exports and imports are not necessarily connected nor are they equal, although the government would like them to be.

If all of the injections are added together and all of the withdrawals are added together then a new equilibrium condition can be established.

■ Injections = Withdrawals

   $(I + G + X) = (S + T + M)$

Review Terms

Wages; rent; interest; profit; income; savings; consumption; rate of interest; intended savings; real savings; aggregate monetary demand (AMD); output; equilibrium; withdrawals; injections; direct taxation; gross income; net income; disposable income; government expenditure; imports; exports.

1.6   The Economic System

The economic problem of scarcity and choice exists in every society and community and consequently a system, an economic system, is required to solve this problem. A number of theories exist as to the best way to solve this problem and these theories are subject to great debate. Possibly two of the most widely recognised and extreme theories revolve around the works of Karl Marx (1818-1883) and Adam Smith (1723-1790).

Karl Marx looked at the evolution of the economic system of production. He believed that if the captalist system was an initial or natural state, this would create a polarisation with exceptionally rich employers and extremely poor workers. This situation, he believed, would ultimately lead to the collapse of capitalism and the emergence of a planned or command economy in which all of the factors of production are owned by the state. The logical conclusion to the work of Marx is that all systems will ultimately move towards a planned economy.

In that planned economy, Marx maintained that the people in the society compose the state, and the state makes decisions regarding which goods should be produced, and in what quantities, where production should be located, and the ultimate selling price. If it was agreed that all households should own a car, then the state would determine where the manufacturing plants should be located, and would allocate sufficient resources to ensure that they were capable of making the number of vehicles required. Price would be low, to ensure that everyone would be able to purchase one. Of course, such a decision would have major repercussions on other areas of production, because so many resources would have been devoted to car production, but that is what happens in a planned economy.

The work of Adam Smith, *The Wealth of Nations* (1776), centred around the concept of free enterprise. Smith argued for the simple system of natural liberty. This means that if every individual promotes his or her own interest this will be to the benefit of all society. Smith felt that the state should play as small a part in the running of a nation's economy as possible. Some state activity would be necessary. For example, there would be need of any army, for external protection, and this would need to be paid for, through taxation, and administered through officials, but such state activity should be kept as small as possible. Owners of capital should be free to determine how to allocate resources, what they should produce, together with the quantities, and also price. If the market decided that the price was too high, then the produce would be unsold. He believed that conditions of free competition and optimal allocation of resources could be achieved.

The work of Smith, along with that of Ricardo, Malthus and J S Mill, promoted the capitalist or free market economy as a solution to the economic problem.

Despite the different economic theories that exist and the many diverse types of communities, the solution to 'what to produce', 'how to produce' and 'how to distribute' have created four different types of economy:

■ traditional economies

■ planned, or command, economies

■ market economies

■ mixed economies.

The Traditional Economy

In a traditional economy the decision of what to produce and how to share out the goods and services is based upon tradition, custom and habit. What happened previously is repeated. It could be that the elders, religious leaders or the most productive workers receive the greatest share of output, but whatever has happened before will be repeated year after year. Nothing ever changes.

This is a very primitive agricultural type of society reinforced by religion and superstition. Any change in the pattern of things could upset the 'gods' or bring bad luck. This type of economy has virtually disappeared except in very remote tribes.

Planned Economy

This method of solving the economic problem has a long history and was the method used by the countries of Eastern Europe and the USSR. The best example is China, although this is not a perfect example.

In this type of economy all the decisions are made by some all-powerful authority - a government, dictator or ruling group, often described as the 'state'. The state decides what to produce, how it should be produced and how it is to be shared out.

All of the factors of production, with the exception of labour, are owned by the state. No individual is allowed to own their own house, shop or factory. This creates equality of income, wealth and opportunity. Hence no one can influence output through his or her personal economic power.

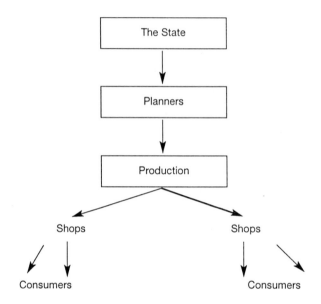

Figure 1.23 The Planning Process

The state, because it has control over all of the factors of production, can plan exactly what is to be produced and how. It is the state that decides the broad policy of what is to be produced. These ideas are then passed to 'planners' who put them into practice, deciding upon quantities, methods of production, materials to be used and so on.

The detailed plans are put into practice in state-owned factories. Goods are produced according to need and choice is not a priority. Clothes are functional and food is basic. In the shops the consumer accepts what is provided and has no choice. There are no means by which the consumers can actually inform the planners of their likes or dislikes. The only information that reaches the planners is that queues are forming for particular goods due to shortages.

Goods are distributed and not sold using prices. Each consumer has an entitlement to a quanity of products. This is done via a voucher system, which rations the goods available. Basic freedoms over what individuals buy, what they own and who they work for do not exist.

The Market Economy

The market economy, also known as the free market or Capitalist system, is the complete opposite of the planned economy. All of the economic decisions are left entirely to the market forces of demand and supply. There is no role for the state or government, excpet as a figurehead. Taxation and the provision of goods and services by government do not exist.

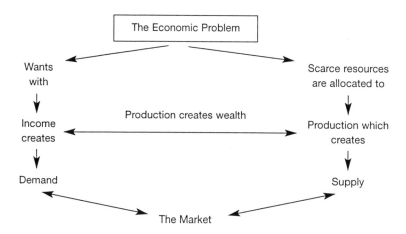

Figure 1.24 The Forces of Supply and Demand

The essential features of a pure market economy are as follows:

- Private ownership of the factors of production, the exception being labour. It is the services of labour that are produced.

- Total freedom of choice and enterprise, within the framework of the law.

- Self-interest as the dominating motive. Consumers are interested in satisfying their needs and wants and producers wish to make as much profit as possible.

- Competition. This is price competition, one of the most essential features. The level of competition should be such that no single firm or individual has the power to influence prices or output. This is known as perfect competition.

- Prices and markets. A market exists for every product and the price mechanism is used to allocate every good or service. If a good or service is not demanded, or no firm is prepared to supply it, a market will not exist.

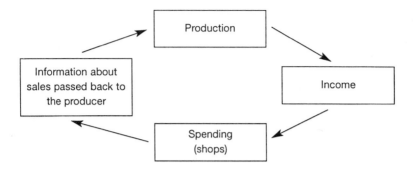

Figure 1.25 Consumer Sovereignty

The consumer dominates this system because the best way for a firm to make a profit is to sell what the consumer wants and to sell as much as possible. Therefore, whatever the consumer wants will be produced if the firms can make a profit. This is consumer sovereignty. The best example of this type of economy is the USA, although this is not a perfect example as the USA does have a tax system, and some state benefits.

The Mixed Economy

The mixed economy is the most common type of economic system in the world today. It is a mixture of market forces: the private sector, state interventions, and the public sector. Every economy is really a mixed economy, even the USA, due to government or state intervention, but the best examples are to be found in Western Europe. The reason for the popularity of the mixed system is due to the problems that exist with both the planned and market economies.

The planned economy does not allow any economic freedom and has to be enforced by a very strict method of control, either through a strong police force or a military system. The actual planning of output is very, very complicated and plans often go wrong. In a democratic society neither of these features are acceptable.

In a market economy a number of features also exist that are thought of as unacceptable. To begin with, a pure market economy is very unstable: it moves from periods of great prosperity and expansion, boom periods, to times of great hardship and depression, a slump period or a recession. The need for firms to make profits leads towards monopolies. The way to gain greater profits is to produce more and become larger and larger; this produces a monopoly. When a monopoly occurs consumer sovereignty disappears and the market fails to operate freely.

A further feature of a market economy is inequalities. The ability to own the factors of production creates excessive market power which in turn creates inequalities in income, wealth and opportunity. The market system only takes into account private costs and benefits; this includes the private production costs of the firm and the private benefits of the individual. Market price does not inlcude the benefits and costs to sociey as a whole, the social costs and benefits. The market ignores factors such as pollution and noise and does not consider benefits unless a profit can be made. Finally the market economy does not provide pure public goods. These goods would not be produced by the market because it is impossible to charge for them due to their unique qualities. Such goods include defence, and law and order.

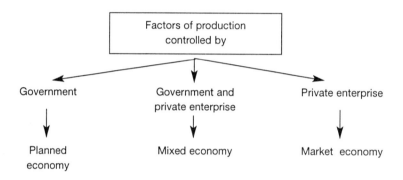

Figure 1.26 Types of Economic System

The mixture of the two types of economy tries to overcome these problems. The market allows freedom of choice for most goods and services. Government or state intervation creates greater stability, ensures a more equal distribution of income and wealth through the taxation and benefits system and produces public goods such as defence. Strict control over monopolies and other restrictive practices helps to prevent consumers from being exploited, whilst government taxes and subsidies attempt to take account of social costs and benefits by changing market prices.

Review Terms

Traditional economies; planned economies; market economies; mixed economies; demand; supply; private ownership; fredom of choice and enterprise; self interest; competition; prices and markets; consumer sovereignty; private sector; public sector; inequalities; social costs and benefits; public goods.

Conclusions

The economic problem of scarcity exists in every community or society no matter how large or small and no matter how sophisticated or primitive. This problem is what gives rise to the many and varied solutions throughout the world.

Political intervention has a great deal of influence on the type of system, but it should be remembered that no system that exists is perfect although many are claimed to be. The aim of every economy is to provide for as many wants and needs of the people as possible. Unfortunately in many societies some individuals always benefit more than others.

Reflective Pause

Advertising : Losing Flash Harry

In Mrs Thatcher's Eighties, the rich got richer and the Porsche got Porscher. So many Britons have acquired this particular status symbol that its status is under threat. This autumn, with the brand image at risk of acquiring an unacceptably wide-boy image, Porsche is the subject of an uncharacteristic £1.5 million corrective advertising campaign.

Figure 1.25 Porsche Advertising the Sexiest Business in Town

In 1977, 600 Porsches were sold in this country. This year the British market will account for over 3,000 sales, making it the third biggest behind the US and Germany. But while sales of Porsche (pronounced by owners as Porsch-er as in 'posher') have matched the car's own famed acceleration. This very popularity runs the risk of erasing its peculiar elitism. It wasn't helped by the ill-fated introduction of the 924 model at a mere £20,000 or so. As Petger Bulbeck, MD of Porsche UK, put it: 'People were buying it who could only just afford it'. Quite.

The trouble is that Mrs Thatcher's decade hasn't been about mere acquisition, but about ostentatious acquisition - if you've got it, flaunt it. And all the research shows that Porsche buyers are what the admen call 'over-achievers', the ones who want to say not only 'look at me' but 'feel my wallet'.

'You don't have to apologise for your 1.3 Escort; everybody knows you have achieved something', says Mr Bulbeck at the Porsche GB centre near Reading. Here Britain's tenth of the 32,000 Porsches made annually are shipped in from Germany for specially ordered trimmings like ejector seats and wings. Mr Bulbeck must be an over-over-achiever because, along with only 400 others in the world, he is awaiting delivery of the new Porsche Carrera 4, a snip at around £50,000.

Despite the fact that the cheapest Porsche, 944, now retails at about the price of a small island off Scotland, demand remains nearly twice supply. But complacency is not in order. Japanese motoring companies, fresh from winning the war for the saloon car markets of the Western world, seem to have taken this as a signal to enter the luxury market.

Bidding to move decidedly upmarket, Porsche has deleted the 'cheap' 924 model and its British operations has sacked its advertising agency of five years. Porsche GB flew six top agencies to Stuttgart to pitch for the 'sexiest' business in town. The winners were Leagas Delaney (Garrard, Harrods, Timberland Shoes), no strangers to persuading those with disposable income where to dispose of it. This month their campaign notifies us of the virtues of buying a German hand-made car from a 'family firm' - in contrast to mass-market, production line Japanese impersonators.

Porsche GB don't particularly want to sell any more cars, but they they do not want to sell any fewer either. They wouldn't mind selling them to a better class of client. According to Tim Delaney at the agency, they need to eliminate what he calls the 'Flash Harry' associations of Porsche owning in the Thatcher years, and emphasise the alleged engineering and design virtues of the car. Delaney too is waiting for his Carrera 4, but is distressed that it has to be red.

Martin Wroe, *Sunday Correspondent* 8th October 1989

Areas for Consideration

1. Explain the way in which the events described in the article can be used to illustrate the concept of scarcity.

2. Discuss, with illustrations, the way in which the 'market' for the Porsche has developed, and is likely to develop in the future.

3. The article explains in a non-technical way the concept of elasticity. Translate this into the technical explanation.

chapter two
The Development and Growth of Industry

The influences that have led to the development of industry and determine its size and location

2.1 British Industrial Development

2.2 Specialisation and Exchange

2.3 Size and Location Influences

2.3 Internal Organisation

This section should enable students to:

■ understand the historical development of UK industry

■ comprehend the concepts of specialisation and exchange, including the benefits and limitations

■ identify external and internal economies of scale and the influences upon

the location of industry

■ appreciate why the structures within industry differ

2.1 British Industrial Development

All societies have experienced industrial change which has influenced its way of life, present and future. It could have been as long ago as the discovery of how to use fire, or the invention of the wheel, so it would be wrong to suggest that at any time in our historical development there has not been change. However, the pace of change has accelerated rapidly in the past few hundred years. When industry was not well-developed, Britain was a largely agricultural country, with a transport system which relied on the use of rivers, the sea, the old Roman roads and local tracks. In other words, transport between the regions was not always easy, and most people did not move around the country. Many people produced the goods that they needed for their own consumption, and so money was nothing like as prominent as it is today. Moreover, the population increased very slowly.

Growth in the Population

Major changes in agriculture in the early eighteenth century meant that greater quantities of food could be produced, and a more varied diet offered to the population of Britain. This extended people's lifespan, so the population began to grow. A larger population meant a larger workforce, while the agricultural improvements meant that work on the land was not available for those wanting employment. A larger population meant an increased demand for food, houses, clothing, etc., and this in turn meant that more had to be produced, and in some cases moved around the country.

Beginnings of Industry

This ultimately led to major changes in the structure of British industry. For example, in the past many people had made their own clothing, or relied on the production of woollen goods in West Yorkshire or East Anglia. However, at this time Britain was engaged in the Slave Trade, with ships leaving Liverpool, taking African slaves to the Americas, fetching goods back to Liverpool. One such good was cotton. It was not far from Liverpool to other parts of Lancashire, where many families were happy to spin and weave the cloth in their own homes. Lancashire was ideal for the cotton industry, as the wet weather matched the needs of the spinners, there were workers available, and also there were sufficient rivers to wash the materials. Thus, in the second half of the eighteenth century, the cotton industry began to produce clothing for Britain's growing population. At this stage, the work was largely done by hand, in the homes of the workers - the domestic system. Machines were being developed, but these relied on water power, and a factory system had not emerged.

The evolution of the cotton industry increased the need for improved transport, but this was only one sector that needed change. Landowners wanted to move grain and other foodstuffs; building materials had to travel from their sources to the areas that needed houses; more and more coal was being mined to heat homes, and so the coal owners were seeking an improved method of transport. As the eighteenth century progressed, Britain experienced many changes as an increased population found paid employment and industries began to develop.

The result was a massive improvement in the country's transport system, particularly the building of canals, which were used in many parts of Britain to connect the developing industrial areas and thus ensure a speedy delivery of materials and finished goods. It also provided work for the growing population and made the country move more and more into a wage earning society with growing financial investments at the centre of the prosperity.

The Pace Quickens

By the second quarter of the nineteenth century, the canals, which had been praised for their speed of about three miles per hour, were now being criticised for very slowness. It was time for further changes in transport. Nothing happened in isolation. Other industries were also changing. Agriculture was changing from wooden implements to iron ones. The cotton industry was replacing wooden machinery with metal, and was also changing from water power to steam power, using coal-driven machines as factories appeared. In other words, the coal industry and the iron industry were growing rapidly, and steam power was gaining in importance. The railway era was about to emerge, and the very building of the railways provided more employment and also helped to expand these other industries.

By the middle of the nineteenth century, the process of industrialisation was gaining pace, and Britain was the world's leading industrial nation. The basis of Britain's economic strength was easy to see. Coal was vital, as it smelted the iron, drove the machinery in other industries, and powered the railways. This meant a huge increase in the number of coal miners and, therefore, the rapid expansion of those areas where coal was to be found - mainly parts of Scotland, South Wales, the Midlands. They experienced an influx of population, and the rapid growth of villages and towns to house the miners. Ancillary areas around the coalfields became prosperous. Near to the coalfields, especially if this was near iron ore fields, the iron industry developed, adding to the size of the population and the local wealth. Again, this was mainly in Scotland, South Wales, and the North East and the Midlands. The cotton industry became firmly entrenched in Lancashire, and was Britain's major exporter. Thus, areas of heavy industry became prominent, towns and cities developed, and much of the population wanted to move to the prosperous regions.

British trade overseas was growing rapidly, and the wooden sailing ships began to be considered slow and old-fashioned. This led, in the second half of the nineteenth century, to the rapid introduction of iron ships powered by steam, and thus another industry was developed - shipbuilding. Of course, Britain had always built ships, but now the location of shipyards was on the coast, near to the iron industry, and so Glasgow, South Wales and the North East also grew in population and wealth as a result of shipbuilding.

Britain prospered as a result of the heavy industries which dominated the North and the Midlands, as well as South Wales and the area around the Clyde, in Scotland. Towns and cities grew as a direct result of Britain's industrial position. London remained the commercial centre of the country, and as such enjoyed expansion and prosperity, but the non-industrial parts of the country became relatively depopulated, and were regarded as poor compared with the industrial North.

Signs of Decline

After the First World War, Britain's economic position had weakened. The thickest seams had already been mined, so the production costs of coal were increasing at a time when foreign coalfields were opening. Moreover, oil power was gaining in popularity, at the expense of coal. Many of our iron and steel plants and shipbuilding yards were out-of-date, and suffering from foreign competition. This was also occuring in the cotton industry, which had failed to re-invest in modern machinery, and was becoming vulnerable to producers in the Far East. The return of Britain to the Gold Standard at the pre-war rate in 1925 meant that British goods were over-priced in the foreign market place, while goods from overseas were competitively priced in Britain. The result was a decline in British heavy industry, where unemployment levels began to rise.

The Wall Street Crash in the USA and the subsequent decline in world trade brought about the international trade cycle, which manifested itself as the Great Depression. Demand for traditional British goods declined dramatically, unemployment in the areas of former prosperity grew alarmingly, and was well over 50 per cent of the working population in the early 1930s.

Other parts of Britain did not fare as badly. New industries such as electronics and car manufacturing had been established, largely in those parts of the country which had not benefited from the industrial boom of the nineteenth century, so that industry in the South East and parts of the Midlands was expanding. This caused a movement of the population away from the regions of heavy industry to those parts of the country where employment was available.

Rearmament in the second part of the 1930s helped the areas of heavy industry, and the outbreak of the war ensured that the mines and foundries continued to run at maximum output. However, the end of the Second World War brought this boom to an end, and the traditional sources of British wealth began, once more, to wither. Foreign competition and the intrinsic lack of competitiveness of British mills and yards saw the gradual closure of many cotton mills and shipyards, followed by iron and steel works and mines. The old industrial areas continued to suffer from closure and high unemployment, and the ancillary industries that had supported the main industries also faced bankruptcy. More and more ambitious families moved away, seeking alternative employment wherever work was available

Development of New Industries

The population of London and the South East and the South Midlands grew in response to the changing structure of industry, which now offered relative job security and high wages, when compared to further North. This decline has continued, so that now Britain has few working mines, a small cotton industry which produces high quality goods, a much reduced iron and steel industry, again often restricted to specialised items. The shipbuilding yards have all but disappeared. In the 1970s, it appeared that there had been a complete change from the position a century before. The southern part of the country enjoyed higher levels of employment and bigger pay packets than the rest of Britain, and there was a clear movement of population to these areas.

The rapid growth of the computing industry was also centred around London, encouraging the belief that Britain was suffering from a North-South divide, with a wealthy South and a poor North. However, further industrial developments have altered this position. New industries, often financed by foreign capital, have moved into areas of high unemployment and have established factories manufacturing electronic items, assembling electric goods and making cars.

Many commercial organisations have sought to move away from the congestion, high rents and property prices, and the high wages of the South of England, and have moved parts of their businesses to Wales and the North, so that, at the moment, these areas are starting to re-establish their industrial positions, though the nature of the industries is much changed.

2.2 Specialisation and Exchange

In poorer countries (Less Developed Countries - LDCs) throughout the world it is usual to find people supplying all their own needs. They build their own shelter, grow their own food and make their own clothes. This lifestyle makes them self-sufficient. They look after themselves and do not need the help of anyone else; they are economically independent.

In the developed nations people very rarely provide for their own wants and needs. Everyone tends to produce one good or provide one service. The money earned from production is then used to buy the other things that people need. This means that people in the developed nations cannot survive on their own; they are economically dependent.

Two of the biggest differences between the developed and less-developed world are that in developed nations individuals are economically dependent and that these developed nations have a good money system. Money is a vital part of any country's development.

If people produce only for themselves then no extra goods are available. This stops people storing goods for the future and so accumulating wealth. It is the accumulated wealth that allows countries to grow rich because resources can be diverse from the production of consumer goods to the production of capital goods. Capital allows countries to produce more in the future and so increase their wealth even more.

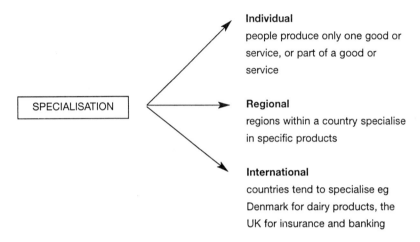

Individual
people produce only one good or service, or part of a good or service

Regional
regions within a country specialise in specific products

International
countries tend to specialise eg Denmark for dairy products, the UK for insurance and banking

Figure 2.1 Specialisation

If individuals specialise it means they either produce a complete good or service or perform one task in the production of a good or service. For example, very few car workers produce a whole car; they concentrate on one particular operation such as fitting doors. Teachers in senior schools concentrate upon teaching one subject.

When people specialise they become very good at what they do and produce more than they actually need. The extra that they produce can then be exchanged for other goods and services they want.

This system works well if people are making bread, for example. They take the loaves that they need and then exchange the remainder for what they want. A problem occurs when people only produce part of a good or if the product is very large and cannot easily be exchanged. A builder cannot take a house into the market place and exchange it for goods and services; civil engineers could not swop a bridge for their wants.

In this situation the only answer is to reward these individuals for their labour. If the reward is in the form of tokens then these can be exchanged for goods and services. These tokens are known by everyone as money. Without money people would not specialise because they could not survive. They need money to provide for all of their wants. Therefore a good money system is vital if specialisation is to take place. Specialisation leads to exchange and the accumulation of wealth and this allows countries to develop and grow.

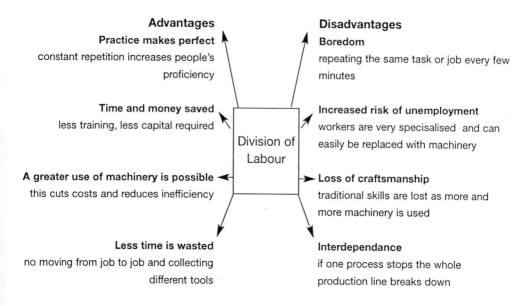

Figure 2.2. Division of Labour

Division of Labour

Specialisation is a process: it means that people concentrate upon producing that good or service, or part of it, at which they are best. Jobs and processes are divided between the workers and this gives specialisation the alternative title of division of labour. The benefits of division of labour were first noted by Adam Smith in his book *The Wealth of Nations*. He described how a pin making factory employing 10 men could increase its output from 200 pins per day, 20 pins per man per day, to 4,800 pins per day, 240 pins per man per day. This was achieved by splitting the process of pin making into 18 different operations with men specialising in one or two operations.

The great advantage of specialisation is that output is greatly increased because everyone is more efficient at his or her job. This allows goods and services to be produced on a large scale. The fact that larger quantities can be produced with the same amount of labour and capital also means that these goods are cheaper. More people can enjoy a wide range of goods and services.

Figure 2.2 shows that the basic advantages gained from the division of labour are economic. They all lead to reduced costs and greater output. By contrast the disadvantages are social, affecting the workers rather than the companies.

Although the division of labour has the benefit of increasing output and decreasing prices it does have its limitations. As previously stated, the division of labour will not work if a good money system does not exist. If people do not accept and trust the money that is given to them they will go back to producing everything for themselves.

The division of labour greatly increases output and so large quantities of goods are produced. This is an advantage if the demand for the good is high. However, if the demand is only for a small quantity then this method is not appropriate.

Some goods and services cannot be mass produced, for example services such as hairdressing and dentistry would be difficult to divide into small tasks. The same applies to general practitioners in medicine; if they specialised even more, each patient would need to know what was wrong with them before they attended the surgery in order to select the right doctor. Some products such as handmade furniture cannot be mass produced. Since they are made by one person by hand.

Specialisation has enabled economies to move away from self sufficiency and subsistence living (with each person producing his or her most basic needs and no more) to more developed economies which rely upon excess production being exchanged.

Review Terms

Economically independent; economically dependent; capital goods; specialisation; division of labour; mass production; self sufficiency; subsistence.

2.3   Size and Location Influences

The major aim of every business is to be successful. Success can mean huge profits, with companies selling more than any other firm or simply becoming a household name. Whatever a firm's view of success it needs to make a profit. Profits are essential to produce a living for owners and keep shareholders happy. If a business fails to earn a profit and makes a loss instead it will soon go out of business.

Economies of Scale

For a company to ensure that it makes a profit it must organise itself so that its costs are as low as possible and so that it can sell as many goods and services as possible. A method of achieving both of these objectives is to produce goods on a large scale. Large-scale production not only increases output but at the same time ensures certain cost advantages. This means that the company can produce more while the cost per unit, the average cost, can actually decrease. These cost advantages are known as economies of scale, the benefits of producing on a large scale.

Economies of scale can be both internal and external. Internal economies of scale are obtained when the individual firm expands. External economies of scale are gained by all firms in an industry when that industry is concentrated in a certain location. The most important are usually the internal economies of scale which are under the control of the company itself, unlike external factors. All six categories lead to decreased production costs for a large firm.

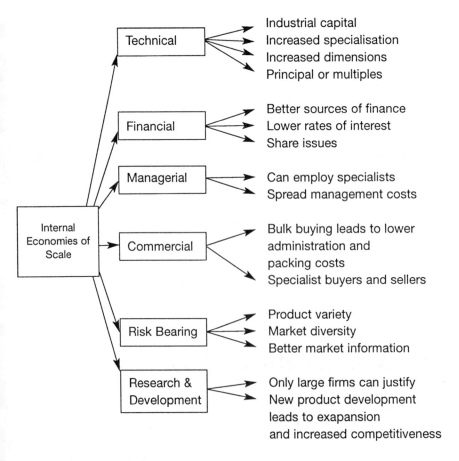

Figure 2.3 Economies of Scale

Technical economies allow the firm to use a division of labour and unit of capital that would not be practical on a small scale. The rule of increased dimensions explains why supertankers and container lorries are used for transport. In the following example, if the dimensions of a tanker are doubled then the capacity increases by a factor of eight, not two.

■   A tanker 300 m x 200 m x 100 m

     = 6,000,000 cubic metres.

If this is doubled:

■   A tanker 600 m x 400 m x 200 m

     = 48,000,000 cubic metres.

Thus carrying capacity has increased by a factor of eight:

■   48 million = 8 x 6 million.

A tanker twice the size would not need eight times the number of staff and even if twice as many staff were needed the cost per unit of oil carried would still decrease.

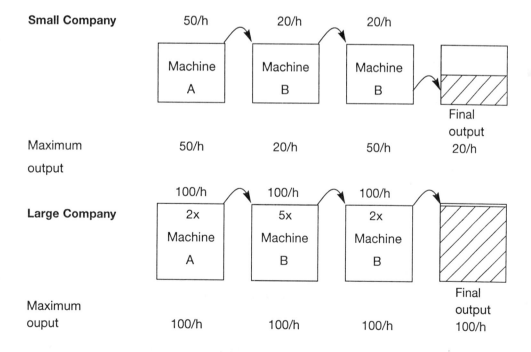

Figure 2.4 The Principle of Multiples

A further technical economy is the principle of multiples (see figure 2.4). Machines often work together, performing part of a task. This often means that production is limited to the least efficient machine. Small firms can often only afford one of each machine type but larger firms are able to employ a number of machines for each process, that is, multiples. These machines can be arranged is such a way that the maximum for each one is gained. Using each machine to its maximum reduces waste and costs.

In the small company machines A and C will only be running at 40 per cent capacity which is a waste of resources and will increase costs. The large firm can afford to buy quantities of each machine. If they buy two of machine A, five of B and two of C all machines will work at their maximum capacity. Output will increase by 400 per cent whilst cost for A and C will increase by only 100 per cent, although they will increase by 400 per cent for B.

Financially large companies have many advantages. Not only do they have access to more sources of finance but usually they are offered lower rates of interest than small companies. It is only practical for large companies to raise finance through shares and debentures so again large companies gain through financial economies.

If output is increased more workers are needed but the number of supervisors and managers need not necessarily increase in proportion. Specialists can also be employed making further cost savings, hence management economies can be made.

Commercial economies exist when firms are able to buy in bulk at cheaper rates and only large companies can afford to buy in such quantities. Packaging and administration costs also decrease per unit as the quantity of goods increases.

A large company has better market information and is therefore aware of changes in the market before the small company. In this way the large company can avoid potential problems and has the resources to diversify into different products and markets. It can also buy from a variety of suppliers. All of these factors are risk-bearing economies which avoid potential problems and reduce costs.

Finally research and development (R and D) is only practical for large companies. Its benefit is that it can produce more competitive products or install new production processes, all helping to cut costs.

Location of Firms

Another very important business decision that also has an influence on a firm's costs is where it should locate its factories, plants and offices. A bad decision can cause many problems and could lead to a decrease in sales or an increase in costs. There are many factors that influence where a firm locates its premises. These factors have changed over time; some that were very important are now no longer vital.

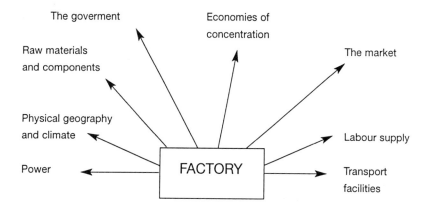

Figure 2.5 The Forces of Location

The existence of a source of power was at one time the most important influence on the location of firms. The main industry that existed was heavy manufacturing and the main, often the only, source of power was coal. It was therefore quite obvious that all major heavy industries should be situated near coalfields.

The situation is now very different. Heavy industry does not dominate the UK economy. Services and technologically advanced light industry are major parts of the economy. Their demands for power are not as great and at the same time alternative sources of energy now exist. The UK has a national grid for gas and electricity and both are clean and efficient. The UK has its own source of oil, the North Sea, and it can be transported using the motorway network. This means that power is no longer a major influence when firms are locating their factories.

Access to raw materials was once a strong influence on the location of industry. The woollen and steel industries had to be close to ports for the import of the raw materials. Again, over time, this influence had diminished: synthetic materials have replaced natural products and the improved transport system has meant that other influences are now more important. For those industries still dependent upon imported raw materials the ports are still a major attraction but many more firms now use components produced by other smaller firms and so their location is a factor to consider.

The nature of the product is still important. Some products are weight-losing, an example being steel. In this case the finished product is lighter than the raw materials and so it makes sense to produce near the source of the raw materials. However, some industries are weight-gaining, an example being beer. The finished product is heavier than the essential ingredients because water is added. Water can be obtained anywhere, therefore it is better to produce near to the market so that the heavy product has a short distance to travel.

Transport facilities have always been important and still remain so. What has changed is the nature of transport. At one time rail transport was the most important but this has gradually been overtaken by road transport and an increasing influence is the nearness of airports rather than ports. For the modern firm it is the infrastructure, the existence of a varied transport system, that is important so that whatever the situation, or nature of their product, they can deliver efficiently at the least cost.

The physical geography and climate of an area are important for certain industries. Agriculture must take account of the contours of the land and the soil; coal mining must be over coal seams; shipbuilding must be near to the water and factories cannot be built on the side of a mountain. It is well known that climate influenced the location of the cotton industry: the damp climate of Lancashire reduced the chance of the cotton thread breaking and so decreased the chances of stoppages which increase costs.

The supply of labour has always been a consideration for firms when deciding where to locate. Labour is a very valuable yet scarce resource. There are many classic examples of firms, and even whole industries, locating in certain areas because of the supply of labour that exists. For example, the car industry located initially in the West Midlands because there existed a supply of labour in the motorcycle industry that used similar skills. The textile industry located in Lancashire because of an abundant supply of cheap female labour, among other things.

A more modern influence has seen firms locate in areas where the workforce has a good reputation for labour relations or where a large supply of unemployed labour exists. This has been shown by the siting of new Japanese car firms in Washington, Tyne and Wear and Burnastone.

The market has also become a very important influence in the location of modern industries. As the UK has moved closer to becoming a tertiary-based economy, producing services, the consumers have become the most important factor influencing firms. There is little point siting banks away from the people and so they are found in the middle of densely populated areas. Many firms that produce perishable foods, such as bread, have to be close to the market because the product does not travel well. It is a feature of many modern towns that bakeries and market gardens are located on the outskirts. All retail establishments need to be close to the market, as do any items that are bulky to transport. Goods that are for export are often found close to a port or airport. The building of the channel tunnel will see more firms locate to the south of London to take advantage of the easy access to France and the rest of Europe. The rail links to the channel tunnel will also attract those firms exporting to Europe.

When an industry is concentrated in an area certain advantages are enjoyed by the firms who are situated there. These advantages are called economies of concentration, or external economies of scale. These external advantages decrease a firm's costs in the same way that internal economies of scale decrease costs.

To begin with, if an industry is concentrated in a particular area then the labour force tends to acquire the skills that are needed: local educational institutions also provide courses. For example, all further education colleges along the coast have always provided courses on tourism and catering. It is only now that other colleges have begun to provide the same courses. In Northampton, once the centre of the shoe industry, there are many courses on shoe manufacture and technology as well as leather technology. This effectively means that those firms situated within the area of concentration have a ready-trained supply of labour. This decreases costs because training is virtually complete and the workers can produce almost immediately.

A further advantage is that the many support services such as banking, insurance, repair, and so on, gain a specialist knowledge of the industry because the majority of their customers will be in that industry. For the time it means that they will provide specialist services for the same cost, but the specialist knowledge will ultimately provide a better and more efficient service.

The concentration of an industry provides many opportunities for enterprising businesses. For example, the waste leather from one shoe factory might not be of much use but if it is from 20 factories then the waste could be useful. The shoe firms who had to pay to have their waste removed the might now be able to charge someone for it. This will turn a cost into a revenue. Service specialists and information services will move to this area, all helping to decrease costs. If the firms are close together they might even collaborate on research and development, again reducing their individual costs.

Finally, the concentration of an industry in an area often leads to that area gaining reputation. The Potteries is known for china and Sheffield for cutlery. Firms can gain from this reputation with increased sales and preferential treatment from banks and other financial institutions.

Economies of scale and the forces of location explain why firms make the decisions that they do. However, firms often make the wrong decision or, over time, situations change. Firms initially increase their size to gain the costs advantages but once a firm begins to grow and goes public it becomes difficult to stop the growth. At this point diseconomies of scale can set in. These are the disadvantages of being too large.

A large firm is difficult to coordinate. The management do not know the workers and the workers feel as if they are unimportant; this lowers morale and decreases output. Customers are faced with a large bureaucratic structure and also feel as if they are only a number. These problems lead to increased costs and a breakdown in the smooth running of the company.

There are also external diseconomies of scale and these occur when an industry becomes too concentrated in an area. An example of this is the City of London. When an over concentration occurs, overcrowding creates a shortage of labour, higher house prices, congestion and pollution which all increase costs. The initial advantages all disappear because the demand for the original location factors becomes greater than the supply thus increasing the price.

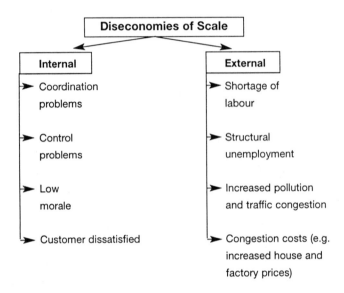

Figure 2.6 Diseconomies of Scale

Review Terms

Economies of scale; technical, financial, management, commercial; risk-bearing; research and development; infrastructure; supply of labour; tertiary; economies of concentration; external economies of scale; diseconomies of scale; external diseconomies of scale.

2.4 Internal Organisation

No matter how large or small a business is there are a variety of widely different tasks that have to be undertaken, such as book-keeping, selling and purchasing, as well as actually making the good or offering the service.

As a company grows, its success may depend on the establishment of a system which ensures that these specialist tasks are undertaken effectively.   This means the appointment of suitable staff and a system which ensures cooperation between the staff in order to achieve the aims of the company as a whole.

Different firms have different needs, but most need to consider the following areas :

Research and Development

This department designs and tests new products and improves existing products. It has to work closely with the production department to develop and construct new products, to ensure that they satisfy legal and safety standards and to make sure that the company has the equipment to make a product.

The Production Department

These are the people who actually make what the company sells. They need to reduce waste to a minimum and maintain the quality of the product. The work can be boring and repetitive, but without production there would be no product, and so the company would not exist.

The Marketing Department

This section discovers what people want to buy, and at what price. It also looks to the development of new products and the updating of existing products, coordinating with the research and development department. It needs to communicate with the production department, as there is no point in deciding that a new product must be made if the production department does not have the equipment or the skills to make it.

The Accounts Department

This department is responsible for all the financial aspects of the company. It records and monitors sales and purchases. It calculates the profits of the company and provides information on all areas which involve the receipt and expenditure of money.

The Personnel Department

This department tries to ensure that the company has the staff to do the various jobs that the company requires. It is usually responsible for staff training and for welfare. Many personnel departments are responsible for discipline within the company. Other personnel departments are seen to have a responsibility for morale within the company, and may organise social events in order to keep up the spirits of the members.

The Administration Department

This department provides a service for other departments in coordinating their activities. It will, for example, ensure that materials are ordered and delivered in time for their production, and will know when goods have to be ready for sale. If there is no administration department the tasks involved remain, so someone needs to be responsible for such coordination. This is a very important area, as there are often rivalries between the departments. Each department tends to see its own work as the most important, and problems are blamed on the other sections. In addition, people tend to identify with their own particular task, and ignore the company as a whole. Someone needs to know exactly who is responsible for what, so that no matter what problem arises, the person who can deal with it most effectively can be contacted at once. That is why the role of coordination is crucial to the success of the company.

The Maintenance Department

This department exists to make sure that the business is properly maintained - floors are washed, offices vacuumed, toilets cleaned and so on.

Managing Director

The managing director is the head of the firm, with authority over all the staff. Very often, this is the person who will fulfil the role of coordination.

Organisation Charts

The structure and organisation of a firm is often depicted as an organisation chart, which can also show the internal hierarchy.

Figure 2.7 shows a traditional type of chart. Companies use these charts to spot communication problems. They show the communication chain and so any communication problems can be traced. Organisation charts also show firms where they may need specialist help and provide the workers, including the managers, with a picture of how they fit into the organisation. Who is responsible for what, and who is in charge of each sector or group of workers can be clearly shown.

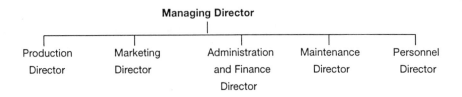

Figure 2.7   Directors Reporting to the Managing Director

A chart on its own is of little use to a company. It is the way that it is used that is important. Figure 2.7 shows clearly that the production and marketing directors are at the same level in the firm but have different responsibilities. Figure 2.8 shows that the production director is responsible for the factory manager and the research and development manager.

Span of Control and Chain of Command

When a company decides upon its organisational structure it has to take into account two important factors: the span of control and the chain of command.

An organisation chart shows the hierarchy of a business, this is the different levels of management from the highest, usually the managing director to the lowest, the shopfloor worker. This is the chain of command within the company. It is the way in which orders or instructions are passed down. Using figures 2.7 and 2.8 together, the chain of command would extend from the managing director, through the production director, the factory manager, supervisors and finally down to the operatives. A long chain of command through which information is passed can create communication difficulties.

The span of control is the number of people that one manager or supervisor is responsible for. In figure 2.7 the managing director has a span of control of five, the production director in figure 2.8 only has a span of control of two. A narrow span of control has the advantage of allowing close supervision and greater coordination, it also improves communication. A wide span of control can improve decision-making and motivation, and may decrease the costs of supervision.

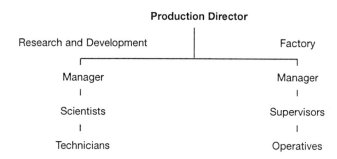

Figure 2.8 Staff Reporting to the Production Director

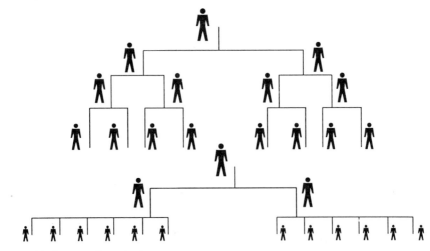

Figure 2.9 Spans of control

Authority, Responsibility and Delegation

It is often thought that these three mean the same thing, but they do not. Managers often delegate tasks to people who work under them. Delegation is the act of asking or giving someone else authority to complete a task or a job. For example, the managing director of a firm is responsible for everything that the firm produces. He or she delegates that responsibility to the production director who in turn delegates the responsibility to the supervisors and operatives. The managing director does not supervise the operative, nor does he or she produce the items: the job has been delegated.

Authority is the power or ability to carry out a task. For example, it is likely that the finance director will have the authority to sign company cheques but is unlikely that the marketing director will have the same authority. Authority is often seen as power.

Authority can be delegated. The finance director may delegate the signing of cheques up to a certain limit to the chief cashier. The finance director would still be responsible for all the cheques signed but would have delegated some of his power.

Responsibility is the duty of an individual to make sure that a job or task is completed properly. If it is not, then it is the fault of the person with the responsibility. If the chief cashier makes a mistake with one of the cheques then it is ultimately the fault of the finance director who delegates the authority, and not the chief cashier.

Authority can be delegated but responsibility cannot.

Organisational Structures

There are a number of factors that can decide the structure of a company. Size is very important. As a company increases in size the chain of command tends to increase.

Changes in technology can change the structure of the business. In recent years, for instance, the use of information technology has decreased the size and role of the finance and administration departments in many firms.

The state of the economy has a great deal of influence on the structure of a company. During a recession many companies need to cut their costs and often layers of management are removed, shortening the chain of command. The opposite is true in periods of economic growth: firms expand and need more workers and supervisors, increasing the chain of command and often the span of control.

Situations such as mergers, takeovers and overseas expansion create very great changes in the structure of a company. All of these situations increase the span of control as well as the chain of command.

Review Terms

Specialist tasks; research and development; production; marketing; accounts; personnel; administration; maintenance; managing director; organisation chart; span of control; chain of command; hierarchy; delegation; authority; responsibility.

Reflective Pause

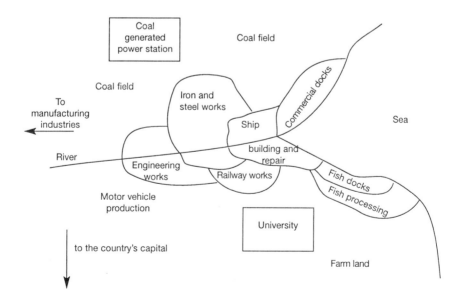

Areas for Consideration

1. What other industries are likely to exist in the area to support those indicated?

2. What transport links are needed?

3. If this map had been drawn in 1955, how much would it have changed by now? What industries would remain?

chapter three

The Economic Institutions

The institutional and organisational framework within which economic behaviour takes place

3.1 Business Organisations

3.2 Trade Unions and Employers' Associations

3.3 Financial Institutions

This section should enable students to :

- explain the types of business organisation in the public and private sectors
- understand the role and functions of trade unions and employers' associations
- explain the role and functions of the main financial institutions

3.1 Business Organisations

There are many types of business organisation, ranging from one man working on his own, to very large firms which everyone knows, to state-owned industries. Together, they make up the business structure of the country.

The Public Sector

Nationalisation

Some industries have attracted particular attention from government. These include coal, gas, electricity, water, the railways, the post and telephones. These industries are vital to the public, and so governments have tried to make sure that they do not act against the national interest. There are two ways of making sure that this does not happen. Firstly by imposing strict rules on the way they behave or by the state actually owning and running the industries. This is known as nationalisation, which became a policy of the UK Government in the period 1945-50. Before 1945, civil aviation, the post, telephones and the BBC were state-owned. To these were added coal, gas, electricity, the railways and road transport.

Nationalised industries are called public corporations, and are run in the same way as any other business, but are responsible to specific cabinet ministers for their activities. It was not intended that they should make a profit but charge a fair price and provide good quality goods and services for all.

Privatisation

Mrs Thatcher became Prime Minister in 1979, and her Conservative Government decided that many of the nationalised industries should be returned to the private sector, where they could be owned and controlled by shareholders rather than the state. It was believed that these industries were inefficient and wasteful and the private sector would eliminate this.

Thus, the public were offered the opportunity to purchase shares in a variety of these industries, which are now public limited companies, for example British Gas, British Telecom, British Airways. This also helped to raise money which the government could use as an alternative to increasing taxation. Until 1980 the nationalised industries employed about 8 per cent of the workforce. As a result of privatisation, this has fallen to below 3 per cent.

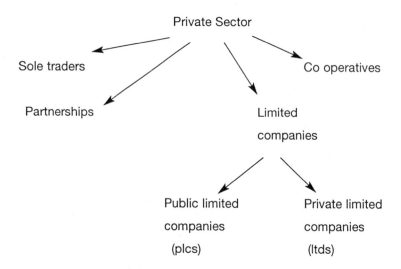

Figure 3.1 The Private Sector

The Private Sector

There are five types of business organisation in the private sector.

The Sole Trader

The sole trader owns his or her business. This does not mean that the owner needs to be the only person who does the work. The owner can employ as many people as he or she wants, and pays them wages. The profits that remain belong to the owner. The size of the firm is limited by the amount of money that the owner can raise. The owner is also responsible for all of the debts of the firm; this is known as unlimited liability. The sole traders may even be forced to sell their own personal possessions to pay the debts of the company.

It is very easy to set up as a sole trader. In Britain, four out of every ten businesses are sole traders, but they only represent 3 per cent of the total turnover of business.

Partnerships

Instead of working on your own as a sole trader you could form a partnership with other people. For instance, a bricklayer and a plasterer may form a partnership to offer a wider service to customers.

The partners will each provide a share of the money needed to start the businesses and each will take a share of the profits. All partners are responsible for all the debts of the business, including those incurred by the other partners in the business. Again these responsibilities are unlimited with personal possessions being at risk if the partnership gets into debt. About a quarter of all businesses are partnerships.

Limited Companies

The main difference between limited companies and sole traders and partnerships is that the financial liability of the owners is limited to the amount of capital that each has put into the company. This is known as limited liability. All such companies must include the word 'limited' in their names, so that everyone is aware of their position.

The companies are legally separate from their owners. The company can sue and be sued; it can enter into contracts, and can incur debts which are not those of its owners. The company is a legal person in its own right.

There are two types of limited company - private and public. Private limited companies are distinguished by the fact that they have the term 'limited' or 'ltd' after their names. They cannot offer shares for sale to the general public. Shares are sold to family and friends. Most limited companies fall into this category. There are about half a million in the UK, but only about 3 per cent are large enough to be public limited companies (plc) whose shares can be openly traded on the Stock Exchange.

In order to protect other businesses, the public and those who want to buy shares, a series of Companies Acts has been passed. These require the publication of details regarding the financial position of the firm and its management.

Limited companies are owned by the shareholders who, each year, can attend a meeting at which they elect a board of directors, who are responsible for the running of the company.

Cooperatives

In a cooperative the business is controlled either by the workers themselves, or by the consumers of their products. The first consumer cooperative began in Rochdale in 1844 and rapidly spread to other parts of the UK. The customers paid a small amount of money to buy a share in the business, and the shareholders elected a committee which decided how the business would be run, and appointed staff to do the work and ensure that their wishes were carried out. Goods were sold at normal retail prices and the profits returned to the shareholders in the form of a dividend, which varied according to how much each spent.

Some societies continue to operate in this way while others have reduced the actual price of the goods, to attract customers into their shops. The number of consumer cooperatives has declined in recent years as a result of competition from supermarkets. In 1950 they had about one eighth of retail turnover but by the beginning of the 1990s this had fallen to one twentieth. Much of the produce sold by the consumer societies is bought from the Cooperative Wholesale Society, which manufactures and imports on their behalf.

Employee cooperatives also began in the nineteenth century. In these, the workers themselves share the profits. They declined throughout the twentieth century, but revived in the 1980s as workers continued to run the firms after management decided to close them.

Review Terms

Nationalisation; privatisation; public sector; private sector; public corporation; sole trader; partnership; limited companies; private limited companies; public limited companies; cooperatives.

3.2 Trade Unions and Employers' Associations

Trade Unions

Trade unions are organisations of workers who have joined together to help each other gain better wages and conditions in the work place. Many years ago when the wages were very low and the hours very long, the unions were much needed. Groups of workers, acting together, were far more likely to bring about changes in pay and conditions than individuals asking for improvements on their own.

In the third quarter of the nineteenth century, unions of skilled workers were formed, and towards the end of that century, unions for unskilled workers appeared. Employers did not accept the unions automatically, and the two sides often disagreed. Employers could threaten to dismiss staff while the unions had their own methods of trying to force their wishes on employers.

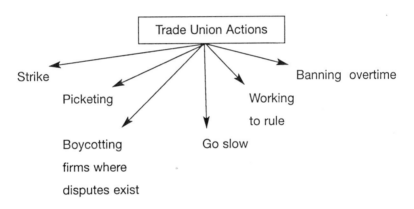

Figure 3.2 Union Action

The most severe of these is the strike, which means that the union members refuse to go to work until their demands have been met. Employers cannot make any money if no-one is working, and they will still have expenses to pay (their fixed costs) so they would be faced with losing more and more money the longer the strike continued.

In the late 1970s and early 1980s, the amount of time lost through strikes grew so Mrs Thatcher's Conservative Government passed several Acts of Parliament which were intended to limit the power of the unions, and so reduce the number of strikes.

Britain had certainly gained a bad reputation for strikes, but this was not altogether justified when compared with other countries.

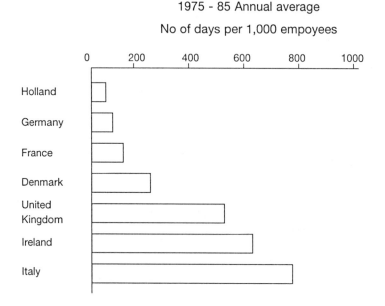

Fig 3.3 Working Days Lost Through Strikes

Number of Trade Unions

The number of trade unions has declined greatly in recent years, so that there are now fewer than 300 trade unions in the UK, many of which do not have a large membership.

The biggest unions such as theUNISON which has over one million members have been formed as the result of amalgamations of smaller unions. This trend towards larger unions has been partly in response to changes in the law.

Most unions are affiliated to the Trades Union Congress (TUC), which is the central body of the trade union movement. It holds an annual conference which decides on general policy although the individual unions can ignore the decisions if they wish.

Membership

The membership of trade unions has declined greatly in recent years, but nevertheless about 40 per cent of workers in the UK are members of unions. Some industries have more than this, some less. For example, most coal miners are members of a union, but the hotel and catering industry does not have high membership. It is higher among full-time than part-time workers, among men than women, and in large rather than small firms.

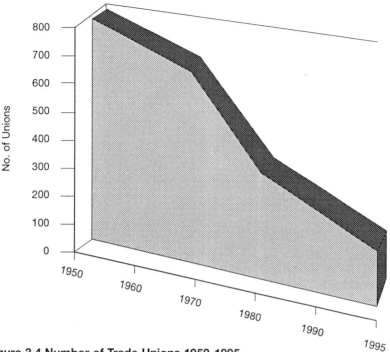

Figure 3.4 Number of Trade Unions 1950-1995

Since the Employment Act of 1990, an employer cannot refuse to employ someone who is not a member of the trade union. This Act made the enforcement of a closed shop illegal. Closed shops still exist but workers can no longer be forced to join a union against their will.

Functions of Trade Unions

Trade unions exist to :

- improve the wages of members
- improve the working conditions of members
- ensure the provision of educational, recreational and social amenities for members
- influence national policy making.

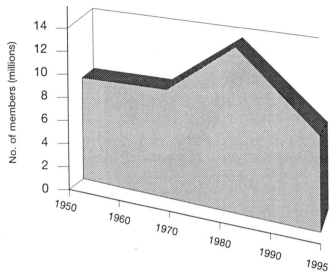

Figure 3.5 Membership of Trade Unions 1950-1995

Employers' Associations

Just as employees have associations, called trade unions, so the employers also have their own groups. The most famous is the Confederation of British Industry (CBI). Most large firms, and many small ones, are members. It has an annual conference, and regularly issues statements on behalf of its members, but it has little real power.

Many industries also have associations, to which firms within the industry belong. They give each other support and encouragement but, again, they do not appear to have much real power.

Review Terms

Trade unions; strike; picketing; go slow; work to rule; overtime ban; Trades Union Congress; closed shop; Confederation of British Industry.

3.3 The Financial Institutions

As the economy has developed, a whole range of specialist financial institutions has emerged to ensure the financial system works easily and smoothly.

The Commercial Banks

These are institutions that collect money from the general public, look after that money, and use it by lending to others who may need it. Mergers have left four major commercial banks in the UK, Barclays, Lloyds/TSB, Midland (HSBC) and National Westminster (Natwest). There are several smaller banks, such as the Bank of Scotland. All these are sometimes called high street banks, because you can find one in the main street of every town.

The role of a commercial bank is to hold money in accounts for its customers and offer a variety of services. These include:

■ loans and overdrafts, provided that the bank is satisfied that you will be able to repay them

■ cheque books, standing orders and direct debits, to make payments easier

■ security facilities, including night safes for businesses and strong rooms for the safe keeping of valuables

■ exchanging currency for holiday makers and businesses dealing with foreigners

■ financial advice

■ executor and trustee services to handle estates after death.

Merchant Banks

Originally these were firms specialising in the export of British goods. This involved the sending of money from one country to another, and the merchants gained a reputation for trustworthiness. Their bills of exchange were therefore always accepted. As trade developed, other trading companies appeared, but their bills of exchange were not always so readily accepted, so the original merchants began to do this for commission. In this way, the established merchants became bankers specialising in bills of exchange. Merchant banks still deal in bills of exchange, the issue of new shares and securities, and act as advisors to large companies.

Building Societies

Like the commercial banks, the number of building societies has fallen as a result of mergers. The main function of building societies is to loan money to individuals to purchase their own homes. This accounts for about 80 per cent of the combined funds of these societies.

The borrower obtains a mortgage from the society. This is a loan. The borrower pays interest on the loan, and repays the loan and the interest over periods as long as 25 years. If the borrower fails to pay, the society can take over the house and sell it to someone else to recover the money owed.

Building societies obtain the money that they loan out by encouraging people to save with them. They pay interest on these savings but charge a greater rate of interest on the mortgages they give. This creates a profit for the building society.

Building societies are now able to do much more than just loan money for house purchase. They offer personal loans, cheque books and credit cards, and in many ways act like commercial banks. Indeed, there is increasing competition between commercial banks and building societies, and the distinction between them is starting to disappear. The second largest building society, the Abbey National, became a bank in 1989 and in 1994 the Halifax and Leeds Permanent Building Societies announced that they were to merge, and later converted to a bank.

Insurance Companies

Insurance companies accept payments, known as premiums, from individuals or companies, and in return agree to pay any financial loss from particular risks,such as fire or theft. The premium is based upon the chance of the risk actually happening, and so is based upon very precise statistical evidence. Some risks may never happen; you may not have an accident whilst driving your car. However it is possible to insure your life, and it is certain that you will eventually die.

Life insurance allows an individual to make sure that, on his or her death, the relatives will have enough money. Life insurance companies have data on all types of people, and their likely life expectancy and so can fix a suitable premium.

The Bank of England

The Bank of England was founded in 1694 to lend money to the government. It is now the central bank of the UK, and was nationalised in 1946. It has three key activities: banker, market operator and policy maker.

As a Banker

It acts as the government's bank. The income of the state is held in the public accounts section of the Bank of England. The government uses this to pay for its expenditure. It acts as a bank to the commercial banks, all of which have accounts at the Bank of England.

- it acts as a bank to foreign central banks
- it acts as a bank to a few wealthy private customers
- it manages the currency of the country, issuing notes and coins
- it is the registrar of government stocks
- it serves the national debt.

As a Market Operator

- it controls the market for short-term loans
- it controls interest rates
- it influences lending policies of the commercial banks by open market operations.

It manages the nation's foreign exchange controls, which are held in the exchange equalisation account. It can buy and sell currency on the foreign exchange markets of the world to maintain the value of sterling.

As a Policy Maker

- it advises the treasury on the economic state of the country
- it has an international role with the IMF, etc.

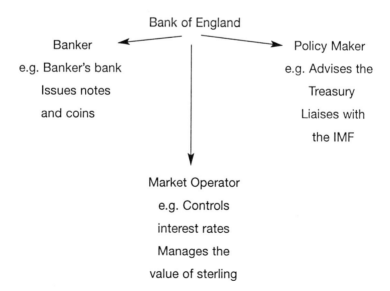

Figure 3.6 The Role of the Bank of England

The Stock Exchange

The Stock Exchange deals with the buying and selling of existing shares in public limited companies and securities issued by the British and foreign governments. It is important to remember that the money coming from the sale of a share that has already been issued goes to the owner of the share, and not to the company.

The value of the share reflects what buyers think about a company. If the price of a share is rising, then buyers think that the company is doing well. If it is falling, then buyers have less confidence in the state of the company.

Review Terms

Commercial banks; merchant banks; bills of exchange; loans; overdrafts; chequebooks; security facilities; currency; financial advice; executor and trustee services; building societies; insurance companies; the Bank of England; the Stock Exchange; securities.

Conclusion

The development of any economic system is dependent upon a sound financial system. It is money, and the institutions to supplement and facilitate the money system, that allows societies to endure beyond the level of subsistence living.

As we move away from a subsistence existence, the opportunity to provide for others arises. Private enterprise, the providing for others whilst enhancing ones own wealth, is an acceptable part of all developed economies. Such is the urge to make a profit that employees need protection again unscrupulous employers.

In the late 1970s the UK encountered a situation where the trade unions were dominant and created problems throughout the economy. In the 1990s the pendulum appears to have swung in the opposite direction and the trade unions have lost much of their power and influence. The situation of the late 1990s may never return but the question is, would we want it to?

Reflective Pause

The Story of a Frustrated Businessman

In years gone by, if you wanted to borrow money, then you went to your bank. The manager was a much respected figure in the community, and he had the power to lend money, so any visit was a serious and formal affair. However, the manager knew you, and knew all about your past record so he make informed decisions on the services he could provide. There was no wonder that he was so respected in the community.

No-one questioned the role of the banks. They took your savings and paid you a rate of interest, and used those savings to loan to other people, who were charged a higher rate of interest. The difference was their profit.

Many people have the same view of banks today. No doubt, students are taught that loan capital is to be obtained from the banks. It is a pity that the banks do not see themselves in this light. They spend most of their time trying to sell you pensions or insurance. If you go to the bank to borrow money for a holiday, a personal loan may well be available, but if you want to improve your business, then life is more difficult. You will have no joy from your manager. Business accounts are held in far away places, with so-called business account managers, who you never meet, and who seem to change at regular intervals. They know nothing about you, or your particular circumstances, and seem more interested in security than prospects. I had always though that profit was connected to risk.

I work for myself because I think that I can make more money than by working for someone else, but the risk is that I may not succeed, and make nothing. A bank may have many customers who wish to borrow money, and some of them may well default on the loan. It is easy to understand that the riskier the loan, the higher the rate of interest that should be charged. Equally, some business proposals are clearly doomed to failure, and so a loan request will be denied.

I invented a device which I patented, and tested with experts in the field. They were all most impressed, and gave written reports commending the invention. I needed £10,000 to complete the development, so I went to my bank, which I had used for almost 20 years. I saw a young lady who I had never met before, and showed her my patent, the cost of assembling the gadget, the likely size of the market and the recommendations. She rejected my request for a loan.

She did not explain to me why, or what I should do to improve my proposal, but suggested that I saw a business consultant to prepare a business plan. I told her that to do this would cost money, which I did not have, but she was not impressed with my argument. What more can I do?

Areas for Consideration

Consider this condemnation of the banking system. The basis of the accusation is a familiar one in recent years.

1. In particular, why has the structure of banks changed so much?

2. Is there any truth in the comments?

3 If there is, what does this suggest about the ability of businesses to develop?

4. Where could this inventor find loan capital?

chapter four

The Governmental Framework

The framework of government which influences the environment in which our econonmic behaviour takes place

4.1 The Role of Central and Local Government

4.2 Taxation in the UK

4.3 The European Union and other International Institutions

This section should enable students to:

- understand the role and functions of local and central government

- outline the varieties of taxation in the United Kingdom and differentiate between progressive, regressive and proportional taxation

- identify the main international trade groupings with particular reference to the European Community

- understand the basis of central and local government expenditure

4.1 The Role of Central and Local Government

It seems an obvious statement, but the role of government is to govern and, no matter what type of society is being considered, the statement remains true. In the UK the role of the government has changed quite considerably over the years; a greater responsibility for the wellbeing of the population has been accepted by the government.

There have always been rules, so the need for some type of agency to uphold these rules has existed (the police); there has always been a need to protect society from outside attack, so some form of security system has been needed (the army, airforce and navy). People are required to organise all of this, so an administration has existed. People need to be paid for such activities, so there has always been some form of taxation.

The Role of Central Government

The development of the government's responsibilities is a matter of history and is well documented. These responsibilities fall into four distinct areas.

The Provision of Essential Public Services

This is the most basic government function, and cannot be performed by anyone else. It involves the maintenance of the head of state, the legislative system and provision for law and order and external security.

The Control of Sectors of the Economy

This can be for economic, social or strategic reasons. It may mean that some industries receive financial support, or they may be state owned, such as the postal service. The amount of government contol is a political matter, and different parties have different views on the extent of government involvement.

The Pursuit of Social Policies

This can involve the amount and nature of expenditure on social services, such as education and health.

The Control of the Economy as a Whole

This includes the maintenance of employment, economic growth, and the balance of payments.

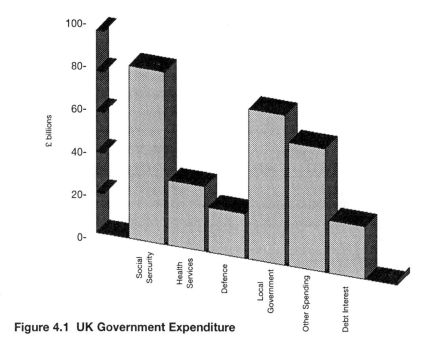

Figure 4.1 UK Government Expenditure

The Role of Local Government

Local government is responsible for activities that are local rather than national. However, local authorities have to act within a framework of rules laid down by central government.

The main areas of concern to local authorities include :

■ consumer protection, which means ensuring that all the consumer laws and trading standards are obeyed

■ education, which means the operation of a system created by central government, and largely involves the building and maintenance of the schools, the payment of staff and the provision of equipment.

■ environmental health services (pest control, waste disposal, etc.)

■ leisure facilities, which will include the running and maintenance of parks and leisure centres

■ libraries and museums

■ personal social services for the elderly, in firm and less able-bodied.

■ planning permission for new buildings, or the change of use of existing ones

■ police and fire services

■ the maintenance, but not construction of roads

■ the provision of housing

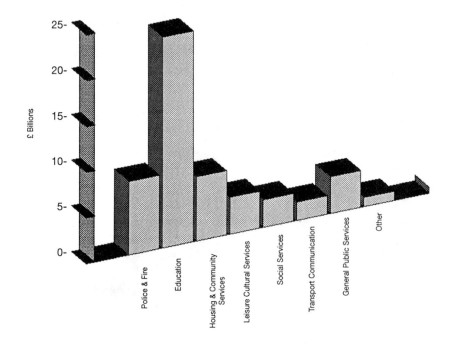

Figure 4.2 Local Government Expenditure

4.2 Taxation in the UK

Central Government Revenue

In order to pay for its activitives, the government has to obtain money from somewhere. The income of the government is called revenue and comes from the general public in the form of taxation. There are two types of taxation: direct and indirect.

Direct Taxation

This is so called because the individual pays the money directly to the revenue authorities.

Income Tax

This is a tax on the income of individuals and firms, and provides the UK government with about one third of its income. Every individual is given a non-taxable allowance which varies according to factors such as marital status. This is subtracted from a person's earnings to leave a taxable income. The first part of the earnings is taxed at 20 per cent. The next is taxed at 23 per cent and any earnings over that are taxed at

40 per cent. This means that the more a person earns, the higher proportion of income is paid in tax. This is known as progressive taxation.

If everyone paid at exactly the same rate, and there were no personal allowances, everyone would pay the same proportion of their income as taxation. This is known at proportional taxation. Regressive taxation is the term applied when the more a person earns, the smaller the proportion of taxation is paid.

National Insurance Contributions

These are intented to help pay for social security benefits. They are earnings related and are charged as a percentage of income.

Capital Gains Tax

This is a tax on the profit that a person make from selling assets. Not all assets are included. The sale of a private house, for example, would not be considered for tax purposes, and gains below a limit are ignored. The gain is added to a person's income and taxed at the appropriate rate.

Inheritance Tax

This is the taxation of the wealth of someone who has died. It is charged at the rate of 40 per cent on estates over a particular value - at the moment about £230,000.

Corporation Tax

This is a tax on the profits made by companies, in the same way as income tax. The rate is fixed in the Budget.

Indirect Taxation

These are taxes on expenditure and so are paid by the individual to the provider of the goods or services that are taxed. As most items are taxed, this is not likely. Such taxes tend to be regressive, as they take a higher proportion of the income of the poor than the rich.

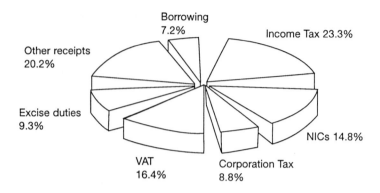

Figure 4.3 UK Central Government Revenue

Customs Duty

This is imposed on goods imported from outside the European Union.

Excise Duty

This is imposed on goods such as petrol, tobacco and alcohol as a separate tax and produce about one third of total revenue from indirect taxation.

Value Added Tax (VAT)

This a general expenditure tax imposed on most goods, except food, and many services. The UK was obliged to introduce this system of taxation as part of its membership to the European Union. As far as the consumer is concerned, VAT is a percentage, currently 17.5 per cent, which is added to the cost price of a good or service. However, the process is rather more complicated, as VAT is charged at every part of the manufacturing process, as in the following example.

Suppose a sculptor buys a lump of rock from a quarry:

- The quarry charges the sculptor £1,000 plus 17.5% VAT = £1,175.

- The sculptor works on the rock and creates a sculpture of Mrs Thatcher.

- He sells it to a museum for £10,000 plus 17.5% VAT = £11,750.

- The quarry has produced a piece of rock which cost nothing, and was sold for £1,000; £1,000 was therefore added to the value of the rock, and so the quarry must pay £175 in VAT.

- The sculptor bought the rock for £1,000 (+VAT) and sold it, after work, for £10,000 (+ VAT); he has added £9,000 to the value of the rock, and so he must pay £1,575 in VAT.

■ If the museum were to sell the sculpture to a grateful nation for £20,000 (+ VAT), then the museum would have added £10,000 to its value, and so would have to pay £1,750.

Other Forms of Income

These include income from loans that the government may have made, rent from Crown lands, and charges for goods and services such as medical prescriptions and dental treatment.

On the other hand, the goverment may itself have to borrow money. This is known as the public sector borrowing requirement.

Local Government Revenue

Central government provides about three quarters of the money needed by local government in the form of grants and also imposes spending limits. The rest of the money is raised by the local authorities themselves.

Council Tax

Domestic properties are valued and placed into one of eight categories, according to their value, and the same amount of council tax is paid by the owner of each property in a band. Single occupants pay 25 per cent less, and people on low incomes also pay reduced amounts.

The Uniform Business Rate

Business property is valued and the central government charges a proportion of that value each year. This is distributed to the local authorities according to their populations.

Review Terms

Direct taxation; income tax; non-taxable allowance; taxable income; progressive taxation; proportional taxation; regressive taxation; National Insurance contributions; Capital Gains Tax; Inheritance Tax; Corporation Tax; indirect taxation; customs duty; excise duty; Value Added Tax; PSBR; council tax; Uniform Business Rate.

4.3   The European Union and other International Institutions

The European Union

Origins

The Second World War left the countries of Europe needing to rebuild the homes and industrial buildings that had been destroyed. The production of industry also had to be changed, from the needs of wartime to those of peace. This was made more diffficult by the fact that the war had been expensive, so that no country had enough money to make all the changes as quickly as they would have liked. Some of the countries of Europe decided to help each other, in order to speed up the process of recovery.

In 1948, Belgium, Holland and Luxemburg established economic links and these three joined with France, Italy and (West) Germany in 1952 to form the European Coal and Steel Community. This established a unified market in coal and steel for the six countries.

In 1956, the same six countries signed the Treaty of Rome to found the European Economic Community which is now called the European Union. The aim was to move towards the elimination of tariffs among the members, together with identical import duties for other countries.

The UK did not want to joint at this stage, partly because of a desire to maintain independence from other countries, and partly through ties with the Commonwealth. Instead, the UK became involved in the establishment in 1960, of the European Free Trade Association, with Austria, Denmark, Norway, Sweden, Portugal and Switzerland. Finland joined later. The aim was the abolition of tariffs between member countries, but without the aim of a common import duty. This satisfied the desire of the UK to offer preference to Commonwealth goods. However, trade with the Commonwealth declined, and the economies of the members of the European Community prospered, so the UK applied for membership in 1962, but was rejected. Denmark, Ireland and the UK joined in 1973. Greece became a member in 1986, Portugal and Spain in 1986, and Austria, Finland and Sweden in 1995.

The Structure of the European Union

The European Commission

This body consists of 17 commissioners appointed by the member governments; one each of the smallest countries, and two from the five largest. It administers European Union policy, including the finances.

The European Council of Ministers

The Council of Ministers decides the policy of the European Union. One representative from each country attends. The representative will vary according to the subject under discussion, to ensure that those attending have a grasp of the issues. The heads of states will attend if the issue is of real importance.

The European Parliament

Each country elects members. It does not make major decisions, but it does have to pass the budget of the European Union, and so it does have some power. In 1979, the European Parliament delayed the budget, and it could use this as a bargaining tool once again.

The European Court of Justice

This deals with matters of European Union Law

The European Union as a Trade Group

The Treaty of Maastricht was signed in 1992. Its aim was to move the members towards full economic union, with a single currency. This did not prove to be popular with the people of many of the member countries. In fact, the Danes rejected the Treaty in a referendum, and so it is uncertain if the measures will be implemented.

The Single European Act

This was introduced in 1992, and aimed to create a single market within the European Union by ensuring the free movement of people and goods within the Union.

The General Agreement on Tariffs and Trade (GATT)

Most of the countries of the world, including the UK, are members of GATT. The main aim is to lower tariffs between members to encourage trade. This is done by protracted bouts of negotiation known as 'rounds' and has proved to be very successful.

The International Monetary Fund (IMF)

This was formed in 1945, and membership was open to all countries in the world. Most are now members. The aims were to encourage world trade and international monetary cooperation by keeping foreign exchange rates stable. To this end, each member made a financial contribution which could be loaned to any member that needed to borrow in order to avoid currency movements.

The International Bank for Reconstruction and Development (IBRD)

This is sometimes called the World Bank. It has funds provided by the developed nations and makes loans, especially to less developed countries, for particular projects intended to improve economic and living standards.

Review Terms

European Coal and Steel Community; Treaty of Rome; European Economic Community; European Union; tariffs; European Free Trade Association; European Commission; European Council of Ministers; European Parliament; European Court of Justice; Single European Act; GATT; IMF; World Bank.

Reflective Pause

Greenley Borough Council

Greenley was a traditional fishing port, with a population of about 100,000. The decline in fishing meant that unemployment was higher than the national average. Four years ago, it was 5 per cent above the national figure, but was now only 2 per cent over, as a result of the relocation of a food processing plant to the area. This had created 625 extra jobs.

The harbour was in need of modernisation, and this would cost about £15m. The European Union's Regional Development Fund would contribute £5m of this, but the Borough Council needed to provide the balance. It was commonly believed that the work would revitalise the fishing industry, attract other commercial seafaring activities, and also create a marina which would greatly encourage tourism.

The town was also faced with poor quality and ageing council housing, and long waiting lists for housing. It would cost £10m to restore existing housing and build sufficient new accommodation to meet current needs.

Leisure facilities were inadequate, and the result was vandalism and petty crime. Expenditure of £1m would be needed to offer the population the variety of leisure activities which would satisfy demand, especially amongst the younger generation, who were becoming increasingly unhappy with the town. In addition, there was a large number of old people, and the facilitites for them were inadequate. £500,000 was needed to address this issue.

The trouble was that to increase the rates would cause dissatisfaction. Local elections were imminent, and higher rates might result in the ruling party losing seats. Moreover, the wealthier residents might leave the area, and thus reduce total income.

Areas for Consideration

1. What are the possible actions the council should take?
2. What are the consequences of such actions?

chapter five

The Decision Makers

The formal constitutional framework and an examination of other individuals and groups who may impinge upon the decision-making process and so influence economic decisions

5.1 The Formal System

5.2 Other Influences

This section should enable students to :

- understand the process of government and debate the nature of the democratic process
- identify some of the external influences upon decision making
- understand the nature and intentions of pressure groups
- question the total objectivity of the media

5.1 The Formal System

Decisions taken by government affect the lives of the country's citizens regularly and profoundly. A rise in interest rates, for example, will cost every borrower and potential borrower more money, so that their available spending money will decline. This may well mean that they are able to buy fewer goods, which means that less will be sold. Of course, the likely result is that less will be made, so fewer people will be employed, so unemployment will increase. More money devoted to education could mean increased taxation, which again will mean that the population has less money to spend. Therefore, the question of who makes the decisions, and how such decisions are reached (who influences these decisions), should be broached.

The simple constitutional approach offers one answer. The prime minister, the leader of the majority party in the House of Commons, appoints the best available members of Parliament to the posts within the Cabinet, most suitable to their talents.

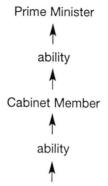

Prime Minister

↑

ability

↑

Cabinet Member

↑

ability

↑

Members of Parliament Representing the Majority Party

Figure 5.1 Political Progress by Ability

The Cabinet make decisions which it considers to be in the best interest of the country as a whole, seeking the support of the House of Commons, with legislation needing the approval of the House of Lords, and finally the Royal Assent ensuring that laws can come into force.

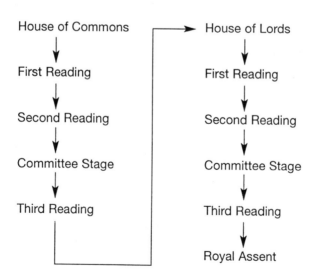

House of Commons	House of Lords
First Reading	First Reading
Second Reading	Second Reading
Committee Stage	Committee Stage
Third Reading	Third Reading
	Royal Assent

Figure 5.2 How a Bill Becomes Law

5.2 Other Influences

The Selection of Cabinet Ministers

The view that Cabinet ministers are chosen according to their ability does not reflect the realities of life, which involve compromise and the requirement to consider the needs of other powerful, and perhaps unelected, groups.

After an election, the leader of the party with the most seats in the House of Commons is invited to form a government, but the very composition of that government may be a compromise. The leader, who has been selected by a vote, is unlikely to be unopposed. Within the ranks of the party, there will be MPs who also stood for the leadership, and they will have supporters. In order to appease such powerful groups, and retain them as allies during the period of government, they need to be offered seats in the Cabinet. The last thing a prime minister wants is personal opposition from within the party, so factions within the party need to receive positions which will satisfy them. Thus, compromise has taken place right from the beginning of the prime minister's term of office.

The party itself may appear to be a coherent unit, but in reality it represents a wide variety of views. The Labour Party, for example, contains a range of members from old-fashioned socialists, who believe in a high level of state control, to those who accept the existing measures of state control and are prepared to work within it. The Conservative Party ranges from those who wish to see far less state control to those who are content with existing arrangements. Leaders of parties need to retain support within their parties, and so need to attempt to unify all of these factions.

Hence, the real situation is that of the prime minister ruling with the negotiated support of the Cabinet and the tacit approval of the House of Commons. As the prime minister comes from the majority party, the House of Commons will support the government provided that the diverse groups within the party are satisfied.

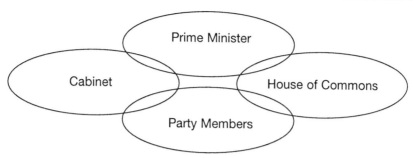

Figure 5.3 The Interaction of Political Groups

Party Policy and the Manifesto

Even assuming that the prime minister has the total confidence of the Cabinet and his MPs there remain some limitations on his or her action. In order to achieve electoral success, the party had to issue an election manifesto. Of course, it is extremely difficult to fulfil all of the promises of a manifesto when in power. This could be because they would be too expensive to the taxpayers, or because they prove too difficult to implement. It could even be because circumstances have changed, and so it is simply not practical to pursue such policies.

Whatever the reason, opponents of the government will be critical, and governments must respond to any criticism, because to ignore it will mean that the government will be accused of breaking its promises and being untrustworthy. Thus the government is restricted in its actions by previously issued policy statements.

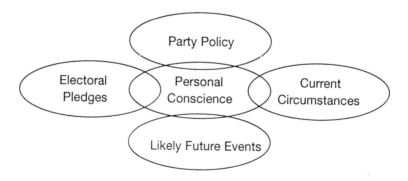

Figure 5.4 Restraints on Government Actions

The Power of Constitutions

In reality, the constraints on government are likely to be even greater than this. members of Parliament, for example, are elected in constituencies, but very few seats actually change hands. One political party or another usually wins a seat. A relatively small number are actually won or lost - most are retained by the same party every year. In other words, a large number of seats are 'safe' - they will be won by whosoever is chosen to contest them on behalf of a political party.

This raises the question of who selects the candidates. In a safe seat, the person or persons who select the candidate will also be selecting the member of Parliament. The next question to ask is what, if anything, they will expect from their MP in return for making that selection

Prospective Parliamentary candidates are approved by the party itself but, having gained the general confirmation that a person is regarded as suitable, it is the responsibility of local constituency parties to select the most suitable person. The constituency party consists of all the people living in the constituency who are members of that political party. Most people do not bother to join a party, so the members are a relatively small group, and not all members are active within their constituencies. A local committee organises political events within the constituency, and a sub-committee of this is responsible for the selection of candidates. The number of people varies from a very small group to the majority of paid-up members but, whatever the process, the local constituency party can select as Parliamentary candidate the person that it wants, and it could be that the views of the particular constituency do not correspond directly to those of the leader. In other words, the candidate and, therefore, in many instances the Member of Parliament, may have been chosen because they do not share the views of the leader.

The Funding of Political Parties

Another important issue is the source of funds for the party as a whole, and also the constituency party, because those who supply the funds may want something in return. The traditional view has always been that big business supports the Conservatives, the trade unions finance the Labour party, and the Liberal Democrats remain poor because they rely on individuals offering financial support.

Such an observation is changing as the political parties themselves change in their approaches to government. Certainly the Conservatives continue to rely on financial support from wealthy individuals and from business donations, and certainly the Labour Party still receives large sums from trade unions, but business donations have increased both to the Labour Party and the Liberal Democrats.

Clearly, those who make such donations deny that they expect any favours in return, and the political parties sound very offended at the suggestion that they would give any favours in return for financial support. Thus, we have the official view. The sceptical view is that if someone gives, say, £1m it could be simply that they believe they will prosper under that party's rule, or it could be that they expect something more tangible. On a regular basis, accusations of favouritism to financial supporters are raised, but there is seldom any proof, and it remains an area of suspicion. Government policy could, perhaps, be swayed by contributors to party funds.

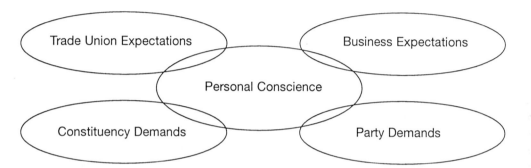

Figure 5.5 Possible Conflicts of Interest for an MP

Rivalries Within the Cabinet

Even if the contributors to parties make no demands, and the constituency parties have selected the most appropriate candidates without expecting anything in return, government may still be under pressure from other sources. Every Cabinet minister will wish to do the very best for the country, so the minister of defence will wish to improve the position of the armed forces, while the minister for transport will wish to ensure that more roads are built, etc. It is the role of the Chancellor of the Exchequer, in conjunction with the prime minister, to coordinate the demands of individual government departments, and to allocate each with sufficient funds. Party political considerations will be taken into consideration, but so will the strength of each individual minister. Some may know the chancellor better than others. Indeed, some may be personal friends, while others are little more than professional colleagues. Will the friend be able to exert more influence, and gain a greater advantage for his or her department? Clearly, that is the sort of information the general public is unlikely to receive.

The Role of the Civil Service

The quality of the arguments presented by each department can help to determine its financial allocations. This means that the ministers will offer evidence to support their requests. The evidence will usually be provided by the administrators in each department - the senior civil servants. The British Civil Service is generally regarded as one of the most honest in the world, and this debate is in no way intended to impinge upon such a reputation, but even civil servants have opinions. If asked to prepare a case for something they disapprove of, there can be no doubt that such a case would be produced efficiently and fully, but there is still the possible accusation that bias could enter into the argument. Certainly, the quality of the particular group of civil servants presenting material will vary, and this in itself can influence decisions made.

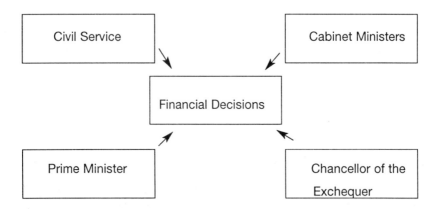

Figure 5.6 The Financial Decision Makers

Spin Doctors

Politicians have for many years taken professional advice about their images, to present themselves to the electorate in the most favourable light. This has meant, for many, a change in hair style, different spectacles which change the appearance a little, to appear more attractive, or suits in different colours or styles, which suggest greater youth, or maturity, less eccentricity or austerity, all according to the impression that the politician is trying to make, and the way in which the image maker believes that such an impression should be achieved.

For many years it has been the youthful look, intended to offer electors a young and dynamic image which has been in favour. In the same way, the traditional upper-class method of speech has been discouraged, as this has been regarded as elitist. If the appearance of the politician can be altered so that a greater appeal can be created, then behaviour also becomes important. The concept of family is one which we hold dear, so that politician a must appear to adhere to old-fashioned family values, and the husband or wife and children become involved in the image making.

Appearances at sporting, social and cultural events, accompanied by the family, continue to present the politician in a good light, and even the choice of holiday destination becomes important. All of this may be criticised by some as portraying the politician inaccurately, but the image makers can go much further. They can write speeches which say what the public wants to hear, in order to increase the popularity of the politician. They can influence the very actions of politicians, so that their thoughts and activities represent what the image maker wants to see and hear, rather than what the politician actually believes.

The Financial Institutions

It is not just the spin doctors who seek to influence political opinion. For most people in business, economic and political decisions may have a profound impact upon their profitability. The wealthiest and largest companies, who employ thousands of workers, may be in a position to influence the decision makers. Certainly, they are in a position where their views are important, and will be heard.

It is evident that when those in charge of Britain's major firms speak on current affairs, their views will appear in the media, and they are taking decisions that affect the lives and livelihoods of many thousands of British people, so it is quite possible that they are able to exert influence upon our local and national political leaders.

However, those responsible for the financial system and the savings of the population may exert even greater influence. Those in charge of the high street banks can decide whether or not to make loans easily available, and so can help to determine the level of economic activity in the country. The major financial institutions such as insurance companies can influence the state of the Stock Market by buying or selling large quantities of shares, which will alter the price of such shares. An upward trend in the Stock Market implies that a government is doing well, with an aura of prosperity, while falling share prices suggests that there is a problem, and the government is likely to be blamed for failing to instil business confidence in investors. Thus, all of those involved in the activities of the City of London can influence the state of the country, and it would be a foolish politician who did not listen to their comments. To what extent the listening politician is influenced by such comments we will never know, but it is clearly possible to ensure that financial options and the implications of a variety of economic actions are made clear to the appropriate politicians.

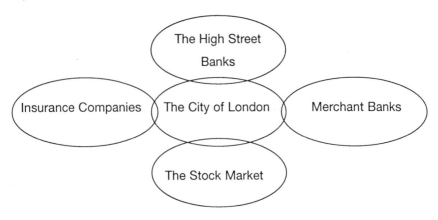

Figure 5.7 The Composition of the City of London

Figure 5.8 The Flow of Ideas from Industry to the Politicians

The Media

Most of the information that the majority of the population receives about current affairs comes from radio, television or the press. Indeed, it would be true to say that most people rely on these sources for any real idea of what is happening in the world. It is probably fair to say that news is usually reported as accurately as possible, though it is through the eyes of the compiler. Anyone who has watched sports matches and then read the reports in the press or listened to the pundits on the radio or television, may have wondered if they had watched the same game. It could be that news reporters give their interpretation of events, which other may perceive differently. Thus, any report has the limitation of the skills of the person making it. In some countries, there could be an official version of what has happened, which may not correspond to what actually happened. However, in Britain, we have what is normally regarded as a free press, so such direct censorship is most unlikely.

Nevertheless, those writing the news reports do have opinions, and may well include such opinions in their writing. The editor of a paper or a programme may actually wish for a piece to show a leaning to one viewpoint or another, and so the report is deliberately produced to offer support for one opinion, or opposition to another. The owner of the paper or the station may wish to encourage particular opinions, and so ensures that staff produce suitable reports. After all, some newspapers openly support particular political parties, and television programmes are regularly accused of showing bias to one party or another, so we can never be absolutely certain that any reporting is totally objective.

The press depends for its financial survival upon advertising, and major advertisers may have opinions that they wish to see expressed in the papers, and may threaten to move their loyalties if such opinions are not expressed. There is no direct evidence of this, but advertisers have the power of their budgets, and no paper can afford to lose revenue.

This is not to accuse the media of misleading the nation, but merely to suggest that, when anyone makes judgmental comments, or presents information, we ask why they are so doing. It is so easy to present the same information in different ways so as to suggest different conclusions. For example, suppose that, over a year, the price index rose by 10 per cent. If you wish to report this as a very small increase, then show a graph as follows :

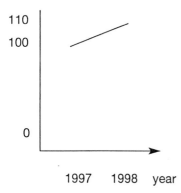

Figure 5.9 Index of Prices

The increase looks small, because of the scale chosen. If this was accompanied by a headline such as 'PRICE INCREASES LOW THIS YEAR', many people would not even bother to read the graph, and discover that the increase was actually 10 per cent, but they would accept the headline comment.

On the other hand, a headline could state 'STEEP ANNUAL PRICE RISE' with a graph looking like this.

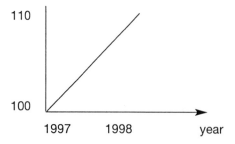

Figure 5.10 Index of Prices

Now the graph is rising steeply, so the headline appears to be supported statistically, and, again, is likely to be believed. Both graphs are correct, but both imply different results, depending on what the person who wrote the report wanted to have the reader believe. The only conclusion that can be drawn is that all information should be read thoroughly, analysed, and the aims of the writer questioned before drawing conclusion.

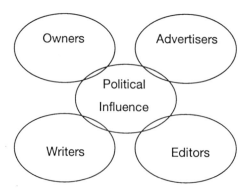

Figure 5.11 Those who Could Influence the Reporting of Events

Public Opinion

In the end, politicians do depend upon the general public because the voters put politicians into power. At least at election time, the views of the population are vital.

It would be wrong to suggest that politicians ignore public opinion the rest of the time, for they always wish to be represented in the best light, responding to the will of the electorate.

There are many groups who seek to influence government in its decision-making process, and the most open of these claim to represent all or many of the public at large. For example, many car owners are members of a motoring organisation. They join mainly because of the protection offered in the case of a break down. However, the motoring organisations speak on behalf of their members on transport issues. To what extent such opinions are representative of the members is doubtful, but government will not wish to alienate the members by dismissing the opinions of the motoring organisations.

All politicians will seek to appear to care about all of the issues raised by groups within our community, as the spin doctors have convinced their charges that they should appear at all times to be caring and concerned, open-minded and sympathetic.

Review Terms

Prime minister; socialists; state control; election manifesto; policy statements; constituencies; chancellor of the Exchequer; British Civil Service; spin doctors; economic and political decisions; financial system; Stock Market; the media; public opinion.

Conclusion

The decision-making process is easy to trace, but the influences upon the decision makers are far harder to discover. It is clear that there are many groups of people who, either openly, in the case of many pressure groups, or privately, in other cases, seek to persuade politicians to listen to their arguments and respond sympathetically. To what extent they are successful, we may never know. In the same way, supporters of political parties may seek to sway public opinion by gentle manipulation or favourable interpretations of certain events. Again we may never know if this has happened, or whether or not they have succeeded.

Reflective Pause

Breathtaking Quotes from the Tobacco Industry

'Smoking and health is an issue that my company and the industry take very seriously'.

(P Sheehy, Chairman, BAT 10/82)

'Despite a never-ending stream of research on the possible health hazards of smoking, there is no proof of a cause and effect relationship between cigarette smoking and various alleged smoking diseases'.

(Dr L Blackman, Director of R&D, BAT 11/81)

'Our managerial ideology lies in our corporate efforts to help make people's lives healthier, more cultural and happier by means of mental relaxation and communion offered by our product and services'.

(Japan Tobacco International, 9/78)

'Irrespective of how many children take up smoking in a year, no one's immortal - everyone dies sooner or later'.

(R Berryman, Tobacco Institute, Australia, 1989)

'Advertising neither entices people (particularly young people) to start smoking, nor does it encourage those who do, to smoke more'.

(Canadian Tobacco Manufacturer's Council, 6/87)

'We did everything we could to sell cigarettes to young people, old people, and anyone we could get. We were always anxious to get more people smoking'.

Emerson Foote, Account Executive on Lucky Strike Campaign, *Los Angeles Times* 24/7/88)

'Marathons taken at a jogging pace may be yet another sport in which tobacco products can not only be seen to be advertised but enjoyed while participating'.

(Charles Adams, *Tobacco,* 9/82)

'We don't smoke that s***, we just sell it. We reserve the right to smoke for the young, the poor, the black and the stupid'.

(RJR executive, quoted in the *Sunday Times*)

Product of ASH

Action on Smoking and Health

Some interesting statistics

1. Death Rates per Million in 1978 in UK

Notifiable industrial diseases	0.02
Radiation	0.06
Homicides	12.70
Road Accidents	126.00

Premature deaths attributable to smoking have been estimated at 50,000 minimum to 95,000. This gives a death rate per million of approximately 900,000.

2. Cost to the NHS of Hospital Treatment in England and Wales at 1979 prices

Road accidents	£75m
Alcohol-related diseases and accidents	£50-69m
Accidents at home	£87m
Smoking-related diseases	£115m

3. It has been estimated that out of 1,000 young men who smoke

    1 will be murdered

    6 will die in road accidents

    250 will die prematurely as a result of smoking.

Areas for Consideration

Examine the comments and statistics offered above

1. How effectively could they be used to oppose or support smoking?
2. What other material would be useful?

chapter six

Unemployment, Inflation and Economic Growth

The criteria against which economic behaviour and government performance might be assessed

6.1 Unemployment

6.2 Inflation

6.3 Economic Growth

6.4 The Standard of Living and the Quality of Life

6.5 Monetary and Fiscal Policy

This section should enable students to

- understand the causes and consequences of unemployment
- recognise the causes and consequences of inflation
- identify the factors that influence the standard of living
- appreciate the differing solutions to the problems of unemployment, inflation and poor economic growth.

6.1 Unemployment

The Problem of Unemployment

Unemployment exists when people are willing and able to work, but are unable to find employment. In such a situation, the state usually offers some type of financial compensation to ensure that those who are unemployed are able to maintain a minimum standard of living.

The main problem with unemployment is that it wastes resources. Labour is a valuable and versatile factor of production, and is normally used to satisfy the wants and needs of society by increasing the output of goods and services. Unemployment affects national output. If 10 per cent of the working population is unemployed, then

10 per cent greater output could have been achieved if those people had been working.

The unemployed clearly do not earn an income, but claim state benefits. These benefits are transfer payments, and come from the government. Necessarily, the higher the level of unemployment, the higher these payments will be. Government expenditure thus increases, and those who are unemployed are no longer earning, and so pay no taxation. Government expenditure increases, while at the same time income falls, which will cause serious problems to the balance of the budget and the distribution of money to other government departments.

Unemployment causes enormous problems for those involved. Disposable income falls, as benefits are less than wages from employment, and this in itself is sufficient to disrupt the lives of those involved. In addition, the unemployed suffer great social problems, and often feel unwanted and depressed, and this impacts upon their families in the form of general unhappiness and lower standards of living.

The Causes of Unemployment

There are many different explanations of the causes of unemployment, and a variety of different definitions, but all of these include the same basic points. The life cycle of any product is determined by the demand for it. Once society decides that it no longer wishes to purchase a product, then it will cease to be made, and those employed in its manufacture will either find alternative employment or will become unemployed. The demand for a product may not be international, so that a product may be wanted in one country, but not in another. Industries are in different stages of development in different countries. The shipbuilding industry, for example, was once one of Britain's strongest sectors, but is now in serious decline. That does not mean that no-one needs ships, but rather that other countries have become more proficient in their manufacture. The decline of any industry creates structural unemployment - unemployment which is created by a change in the structure of the economy.

Ever since the invention of the wheel, there have been regular inventions that have changed the nature of employment for some people. Technology changes over time. New and improved products become available, and technology replaces parts of jobs, or in some cases complete jobs, making the workers unemployed. The best example is the replacement of people by computers in offices, and the introduction of robots to perform tasks formerly undertaken by car workers. People who lose their jobs as a result of this kind of action suffer from technological unemployment.

Residual unemployment refers to those members of the community who are unable to work, or who have decided that they do not wish to take employment, either because they are sufficiently wealthy or because they are nearing retiring age, or similar reasons which show that they are not a financial burden on the state.

Such people should be distinguished from the voluntary unemployed, which refers to that group who do not want to work, but who nevertheless draw state benefits.

Frictional unemployment involves those who are changing jobs. This can include students who complete their courses, and secure a job, but have a gap between the end of the school, college or university year and the commencement of the employment, as well as the more obvious time gap as people move between posts.

There is also seasonal unemployment. This is common in holiday resorts, where many people can gain employment during the period when holiday makers flock to the area, but become unemployed in the off-season. This can include hotel and guesthouse owners, as well as the cooks, waiters and cleaners, amusement arcade workers, novelty shop owners and others who benefit from the influx of visitors. There are other industries where seasonal work is a feature. This can include harvest time in agriculture, activities of fishermen and construction workers.

The Trade Cycle

The trade cycle refers to the variations in the levels of business activity that occur in a country over a period of time. In the nineteenth century in Britain, each trade cycle took about ten years to complete. This would be characterised by a boom, with high levels of business activity, accompanied by high employment, a large volume of production, economic growth and general prosperity, followed by a recession which saw falling levels of employment, lower production, reduced economic growth and less prosperity. The recession would turn into a depression, with high unemployment, low levels of production and economic growth, and a general sense of relative poverty. Then would come a recovery, with improved levels of employment, increased production and economic growth, and a buzz of economic expectancy. This, in turn, would be followed by a return to the boom period.

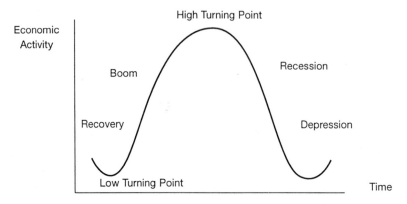

Figure 6.1 The Trade Cycle

The causes of the trade cycle were not fully understand in the nineteenth century, but the work of John Maynard Keynes has made them much clearer to modern students.

When a recovery begins, more people are employed than were previously. This newly-employed group now has a higher income than previously, and so makes more purchases. This, in turn, means that more goods are bought, so more have to be manufactured. More people need to be employed to make the extra goods, and so the recovery becomes a self-perpetuating process until the higher turning point of the boom has been reached.

When a recession commences, fewer people are being employed, and so those who have been unemployed have less income to spend, which in turn reduces the quantity of goods bought. A reduced demand for goods reduces the demand for labour, and so more unemployment results, and again this becomes an on-going process until recovery begins.

This simple version of events does not explain why depression turns into recovery, or why boom becomes recession, but Keynes has produced a more sophisticated and scientific account, known as the Multiplier and the Accelerator.

The Multiplier

If you have received an increase in your income, you may well spend all of it, but others might save it all. Many people would spend some of the increase and save the remainder. This can be measured. The marginal propensity to save, could be defined as the proportion of any increase in income which is saved. It can be calculated as :

$$\frac{\text{Amount of any Wage Increase Saved}}{\text{Total Increase in Wages}}$$

Thus, if someone received a wage increase of £10, and they decided to spend £8 of this and to save the remaining £2, then:

$$\text{the Marginal Propensity to Consume} = \frac{8}{10} = 0.8$$

$$\text{the Marginal Propensity to Save} = \frac{2}{10} = 0.2$$

An important point to consider is that money circulates, and so if one person receives a wage increase and they decided to spend some or all of that increase, others will benefit, because the purchases made will create an unexpected and additional income to those who receive it, and then they themselves will spend it, so the impact of an increase in income is greater than the actual amount involved.

Using the example above, if someone does receive an additional £10, then we are describing the movement of a single £10, and tracing the impact of its injection into the flow of money.

If £2 is removed from circulation in the form of saving, then £8 is spent. The person who receives that £8 will also spend some and save some. If the same marginal propensities to save and consume are used throughout this example, then two tenths of the £8 will be saved (£1.60) and then the remaining eight tenths (£6.40) is spent. Someone else will receive the £6.40 and, of this, £1.28 will be saved and £5.12 spent. This will continue until all of the money is saved, and none remains for spending.

Using these figures, then £10 would be saved and £40 spent. In other words, the impact of giving one person a wage increase of £10 is to create savings of £10 and spending of £40 in the economy as a whole.

The full impact on the economy, therefore, which is known as the value of the multiplier, can be calculated using the formula:

Multiplier = 1/the Marginal Propensity to Save

In the example above, that would be 1/0.2 = 5.

This is a vital piece of information as it allows, for example, the chancellor of the Exchequer to calculate the rate of recovery or the rate of depression, and provides a considerable weapon to a chancellor who seeks to mitigate the difficulties of the trade cycle. It provides a mathematical account of the simple explanation to the movements of the trade cycle offered.

The Accelerator

A simple mathematical model helps to explain the accelerator and at the same time shows why there are changes in the direction of the trade cycle.

Suppose that a factory has ten machines, each of which can manufacture 100 units per year.

Maximum output = No. of machines x output

= 10 x 100

= 1,000 p.a.

Each machine will last for ten years if worked to full capacity. In order to ensure that the expenditure on replacement machines is regular, the company replaces one each year.

This is fine, as long as demand does not exceed 1,000 units per year. However, suppose that demand rises to 1,100 units in one year. The company could ignore the increase in demand, but this is not likely. Most firms would seek to meet the demand.

To make 1,100 units, this company requires 11 machines. Thus in this particular year, the company will have to purchase its customary replacement machine plus one additional machine. In other words, it will have doubled its normal capital expenditure.

The money for this may come from reserves, but the response of most firms to an increase in costs is to increase price. If customers have a limited amount of money to spend on a product and price increases, then the likely effect is that fewer goods are bought. If an item costs £1.00, and an individual normally spend £5.00 per week by buying five, and the price rises to £1.25, then £5.00 will only purchase four units. Thus, the company is faced with the possibility of a fall in demand.

Apply this concept to the trade cycle. In a boom, demand is increasing. Firms try to meet this increase by higher capital expenditure and, as a result, increased prices. Consumers have a limited amount of money to spend, and so the increased prices cause a fall in the number of goods purchased. This, in turn, brings about a fall in the number of goods manufactured and, therefore, a reduction in the numbers employed. Thus, the recession has begun.

Return to the original position. Demand falls to 900 units per year. Now the company requires only nine machines. In this year it would scrap one machine that has reached the end of its working life, and this would leave nine machines. There is no need to buy a replacement, as it would not be used. Thus, capital expenditure is zero, and so the firm's costs have fallen and so the firm could reduce its prices. If customers have a limited amount of money to spend on a product, and price decreases, then either the same number of goods are bought at the lower price and other goods can be purchased with the money left over, or more goods are bought.

If an item costs £1.25, and an individual's normal spend is £5 per week by buying four, and the price falls to £1.00, then either four units are still bought, leaving £1.00 to spend on other items or the £5.00 will be used to purchase five units. Thus, either this or other companies are faced with the possibility of an increase in demand.

Apply this concept to the trade cycle. In a depression, demand is falling to the extent that firms do not need to replace machines, which reduces capital expenditure and, therefore, reduces prices. Consumers have a limited amount of money to spend, and so the reduced prices cause an increase in the number of goods purchased. This, in turn, brings about an increase in the number manufactured and, therefore, an increase in the numbers employed. Thus, the recovery has begun.

Review Terms

Factor of production; working population; payments; disposable income; structural unemployment; technological unemployment; residual unemployment; frictional unemployment; seasonal unemployment; boom; recession; depression; recovery; multiplier; accelerator; marginal propensity to consume; marginal propensity to save.

6.2 Inflation

The Problem of Inflation

The term 'inflation' is used so regularly by politicians and the media that business men and the general public have become aware that when the rate is high then business activity and general prosperity are in danger, and government will invoke measures to prevent this. Unfortunately, the meaning of inflation remains obscure to most people. It is associated with rising prices, and possibly with rising wages, but the real definition of the term is often misunderstood.

Inflation occurs when the levels of increase in prices and wages in a country are greater than the level of production, as this means that prices and wages are greater than the economic growth of the country. If every country in the world suffered from the same levels of inflation, this would not seriously damage any country, but if price increases, for example, are greater in the goods from one country compared to other countries, then the demand for such goods would fall, and unemployment would result.

Inflation, therefore, reduces the value of money in a country as it requires more money to purchase a good or service. This can occur at a wide variety of different speeds. An inflation rate of a few per cent per year would be described as mild, but a rate of 100 per cent per year would be referred to as hyper-inflation or runway inflation.

The higher the level of inflation, the greater the problem created. As money decreases in value, so the less people are willing to accept it, and thus it begins to lose its major function as a medium of exchange. When this happens, it ceases to be money, and so the economy of the country collapses, and people return to either self-sufficiency or barter. In times of relatively high inflation, those on fixed income such as pensioners, the unemployed, the sick and students surviving on grants will suffer, as they will have to pay more for goods and services without enjoying any real increases in income. Those who lend money will also lose, as the purchasing power of the amount repaid will be worth less than the original amount loaned. Those who save money will see it lose value, and anyone employed in occupations with low bargaining power will not be able to source high wage increases, and so will also suffer.

On the other hand, those who have borrowed money, such as home buyers who have a mortgage, will repay a relatively smaller amount than that which was borrowed, and workers in strong trade unions may be able to gain wage increases in excess of the rate of inflation.

The Cause of Inflation

A simple explanation of the cause of inflation is the often used phrase 'too much money chasing too few goods'. This is a very basic description of the two processes which creates inflation – demand pull and cost–push inflation.

Demand Pull Inflation

If there is economic stability within a country, and demand is fairly stable, then it should be possible to look at the demand for, and the supply of, particular goods. A simple diagram would show that a quantity of goods Q1 was produced and sold at a price P1.

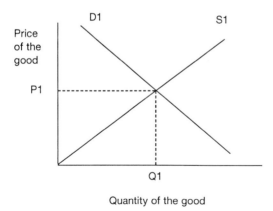

Figure 6.2 Quality Made and Price Charged

In order to make the goods, people need to be employed and paid a wage. Thus, there will be a demand for labour by the firm and a supply of labour by workers.

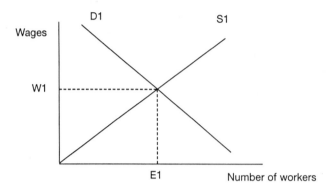

Figure 6.3 Wages Paid and Number of People Employed

This shows that a number of people, E1, are employed, and paid a level of wages W1. However, the two diagrams should be considered together. The firm is employing people to make a product, and so it could be said that, in order to produce the quantity of goods Q1, a number of people E1 are employed. They are paid a level of wages, W1, and the goods are sold at a price P1. This establishes a balance between the factors involved.

A Fall in Demand

If this firm was faced with a fall in demand for its product, then the balance which has been created between output, levels of employment,wages, and prices will be altered. As the diagram below indicates, the net result should, according to economic theory, be a fall in the quantity sold and a fall in the price of the good. This fall in demand for the product reduces output, and so the firm needs fewer workers. Thus, there will be a corresponding fall in demand for workers.

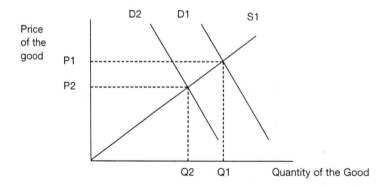

Figure 6.4 Fall in Demand for the Good

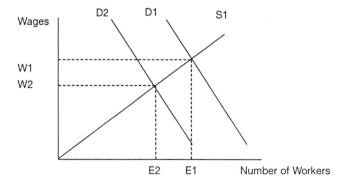

Figure 6.5 Subsequent Fall in Demand for Labour

Thus, a new situation appears to have arisen. The fall in demand for labour, and so the number of people employed, has been reduced to E2, and wages have been reduced to W2.

If that is what actually happens, the output, prices and wages have all fallen at the same rate, and our theory is justified. However, in the real world, this result is most unlikely. The workers are not likely to happily accept redundancies, coupled with wage cuts for those remaining in employment. In the same way, a producer faced with falling demand is more likely to respond by increasing price, in the hope of maintaining revenue, rather than reducing price.

However, if the balance of Q2, E2, P2, W2 is not attained, and prices and wages are above Q2, then they are higher than the level of production warrants, and so an inflationary situation has been created. Thus, inflation can result from a fall in demand.

A Rise in Demand

Let us now assume that, instead of a fall in demand, there is an increase. As far as the production is concerned, this can be show in the following diagram.

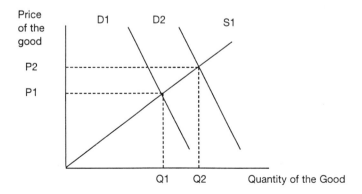

Figure 6.6 Quantity of the Good

The increase in demand means that more goods (Q2) will be sold, and the price will increase to P2. Of course, increased production will require more workers to make the extra goods, so there will be a corresponding increase in the demand for labour.

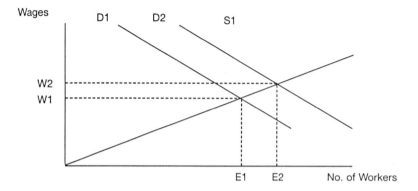

Figure 6.7 Subsequent Rise in the Number of People Employed

Thus, the number of people employed should rise to E2, with wages increasing to W2. Thus, a new balance has been created: Q2, E2, W2, P2. More workers are producing a greater output, being paid higher wages, and the goods are being sold at a higher price. Prices and wages will have risen, but at a rate corresponding to the increase in production, and so this is not inflationary. If this situation happens, then no difficulties arise.

However, suppose that there are not sufficient workers available to increase the number employed from E1 to E2. This could be because the country is enjoying full employment, but this need not be the case. It could happen even with a high level of unemployment, if there are not sufficient workers with the skills necessary for the jobs available. Alternatively, those who could take the might could live in areas far away from the firm, and be unwilling to move.

This would mean that the workforce is unable to increase from E1 to E2, yet, by the increase in demand for labour, those already in employment are ensured a wage increase. Figure 6.8 illustrates this.

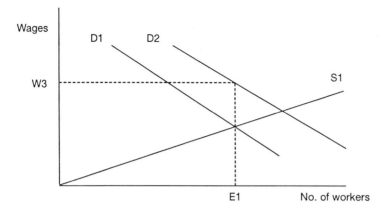

Figure 6.8 Number of People Employed

The new equilibrium position of E2, W2, cannot be attained, and so the number of people originally employed, E1, will take the level of wages available to them, which is indicated by the line to D2. Thus, wages for them will increase to W3. This will impact upon the price and output of the firm.

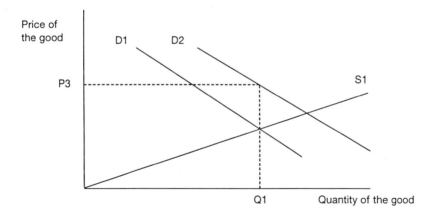

Figure 6.9 Quantity of the Good

If more workers cannot be recruited, then the level of output cannot rise, and must remain at Q1. However, the increased demand means that this quantity of goods can be sold at a higher price, P3 in the figure 6.9. Thus, prices and wages have risen, but the level of output has remained the same, and thus inflation has been created.

Inflation in Britain

The traditional explanations of the causes of inflation have been adapted to explain the reasons for the continued problems.

Monetarist Demand Pull Theory

This theory is supported by such notable economists as Professors Bareau, Fisher, Morgan, Parkin and Walters, and relates particularly to the 1970s. They maintain that successive governments, in order to secure popularity and, therefore, votes, spent too large a proportion of the national income in the following ways.

- By increasing taxation, to meet the extra spending. Unfortunately, this would not be popular with the electorate, and would have been rejected.

- By borrowing the money to support the additional outgoings. This would mean an increase in public sector borrowing, and the consequent increase in demand for loan capital would put up interest rates. This, again, would result in political unpopularity, and would have been rejected.

- By printing more money. This would have had the great attraction of being very cheap, as the total immediate cost was at the Royal Mint, and so would have been the policy the governments often adopted.

Thus, in the face of budget deficits, governments were prepared to allow an increase in the rate of monetary expansion. This meant that the amount of money available in the economy increased, so people were able to spend more, without any corresponding increase in production, and so inflation resulted.

Although later governments have sought to address this issue, the monetarists have not always been convinced that some governments have tried hard enough to limit the money supply, so inflation has continued.

The Institutional Wage Pull Theorists

The early advocates of this explanation were Professor Phelps-Brown, Sir John Hicks and Lord Kahn. In the 1970s Britain suffered from a high rate of industrial disputes. They argued that firms, when faced with high wage demands, had to make a decision. To refuse a pay rise would lead to industrial action, and, therefore, a serious financial loss to the firm. The alternative was to conceded, and a combination of weak management and persistent trade unionists meant that wage rises were regular. Firms were also unwilling or unable to reduce the size of the workforce as a result of such increases, and so costs grew. In manufacturing industries, labour represents about two thirds of the total costs, so any increases in wages would lead to a proportionately high jump in costs. Thus, the wage-price spiral would continue.

Those supporting this view blamed the trade unionists for making unreasonable and excessive demands and, to a lesser extent, employers and managers who were prepared to allow their demands rather than resist.

Review Terms

Hyper-inflation; runaway inflation; medium of exchange; demand-pull inflation; cost-push inflation; employment; wages; price; full employment.

6.3   Economic Growth

Economic growth is usually seen as the way to improve the living standards of the people within a country. Economic growth is the increase in an economy's level of real output over a period of time. Gross National Product (GNP) is the most commonly used measure of an economy's level of output per year. The definition of growth is:

- the percentage rate of exchange in real GNP per capita over one year.

The Advantages of Growth

Economic growth is generally considered to be important because it creates many benefits which everyone can enjoy. A higher level of output (economic growth) provides more goods and services for people to enjoy, providing a higher standard of living.

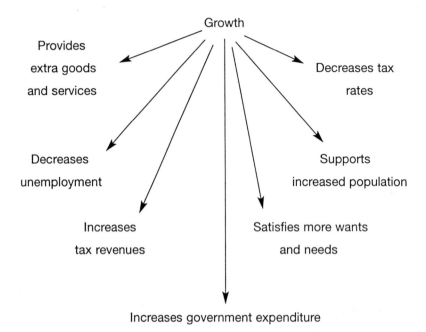

Figure 6.10 The Benefits of Growth

If an economy is growing, that is, it has an increasing GNP, more goods and services are produced. This requires more workers. The level of unemployment is thus reduced and there is more tax revenue for the government. An increase in revenue allows the government either to decrease the tax rate or increase expenditure on schools, hospitals, roads or other public goods. Whatever choice is made the people benefit.The extra goods and services produced through economic growth allow a country to support an increased population and everyone benefits.

The Problems of Growth

Economic growth was always assumed to be a good thing, but this is not necessarily the case. The way that the growth is achieved is very important. In many cases the cost of the growth is greater than the benefits it provides, especially if it produces pollution and waste.

Growth within an economy is not always enjoyed by all of the people equally. Some regions such as the South East of England may benefit more than other regions. This produces an unfair balance in the country and the regions that grow suffer external costs such as pollution.

The increase in output created by growth requires more raw materials and capital. This uses the scarce natural resources even more quickly than before. Many of these resources cannot be replaced.

Growth provides more goods and services but if the distribution of income is unequal then not everyone can afford the extra produced. Again this produces an unfair situation where the rich gain a great deal and the poor gain very little.

An increase in output requires more factors of production. The increase in demand for these factors increases their price and hence the cost of living. The extra capital required for growth initially demands more labour but eventually labour is replaced by capital. This creates unemployment which is a social cost.

Finally, it has been found that in countries that have a very high rate of growth they have also developed a faster lifestyle. This has produced its own social difficulties such as health problems and a higher crime rate.

Social and External Costs

One of the problems of economic growth is that it creates social and external costs, known as externalities. Social costs are those costs suffered by society as a whole due to the actions of one party. This is not a money cost but an opportunity cost. If a chemical factory pumps waste into a river then society suffers. The river is dirty and the fish cannot survive. This is a cost to society as a whole.

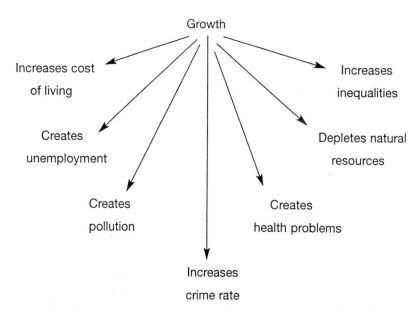

Figure 6.11 The Costs of Growth

An external cost is also a social cost, but is described as the result of an action in a market. Externalities can provide benefits as well as costs.

Unbalanced growth that benefits one area leads to an increase in the number of people and firms within an area. This creates a number of external costs such as overcrowding and pollution, all incurring social costs.

The fact that growth increases the income of many people usually leads to the purchase of more luxury items. One such item is the motor car. Growth usually produces more cars and these pollute the atmosphere (external cost) and create more accidents, which not only produces a money cost for police and hospitals, but a social cost for society to bear.

The depletion of resources may not create a social cost now, but in the future there will be less resources and so future generations will suffer. Growth now is creating social costs for the future.

The result of a greater use of capital, usually associated with growth, is that less labour is needed. People are either made redundant or need to retrain in order to find other employment. Those made unemployed or who need to retrain incur disruptions and hardships not felt by everyone. To such individuals these are social costs.

Growth creates a faster lifestyle which has been shown to produce other problems such as heart disease, cancer, stress-related illnesses, a higher suicide rate and a higher crime rate. These are all social costs that result from economic growth.

Review terms

External costs; social costs; pollution; unemployment; externalities; unbalanced growth; overcrowding; depletion of resources.

6.4 The Standard of Living and the Quality of Life

Economic growth is important because it provides more goods and services for people. The fact that individuals have the chance to enjoy these extra goods and services should improve their lives, their standard of living.

The major reason why governments try to achieve economic growth is to make extra goods and services available to satisfy more of the wants and needs of individuals, and so improve everyone's standard of living. The standard of living, also known as the level of economic welfare or real income, is best defined as :

■ the level of material wellbeing of an individual or household.

Hence the more goods and services produced the better an individual's or household's standard of living. This is why economic growth and standard of living are so closely linked.

Measurement of the Standard of Living

If the standard of living is the material wellbeing of individuals and households, the way to measure it is to calculate the amount of goods and services that are available to each person. Firstly, the amount of goods and services produced by an economy is assessed. This is the gross national product (GNP); the monetary value of all of those goods and services produced by domestically owned factors of production in one year. In the case of the UK it would be those goods and services produced by factors of production owned by the UK citizens.

If the GNP, the value of the output of the nation, is then divided by the total number of people in the country, GNP per head is found. This is also known as GNP per capita. This provides a money value for the amount of goods and services that are available to each individual in one year. This is the accepted measurement for the standard of living.

This is only a monetary indicator of the amount of goods and services per person, nothing else. It relies heavily upon the GNP figure being accurate and the value of money remaining constant. If inflation exists and the value of money changes, other calculations have to be made.

Use the following to measure the standard of living.

■ $\dfrac{\text{GNP}}{\text{Total population}}$ = GNP per head (per capita)

The Quality of Life

The standard of living does not measure the quality of life of individuals within an economy because it is only a measure of the material wellbeing of those people. The quality of a person's life includes far more factors than the number of goods and services they have available to purchase.

Leisure time is very important to most people. An increase in leisure time should increase the quality of an individual's life. The more leisure time people have, the less they work. However, if this increase in leisure is due to unemployment or a shorter working week with less money, it would not improve their quality of life.

Merit goods, such as health and education, and public goods, such as defence and law and order, are a very important indicator of the quality of life. The more zero-priced merit and public goods, and the better the quality of these, the better the quality of life for the people within an economy. People who are entitled to free hospital treatment must have less worries than those who would have to pay for such treatment and may not be able to afford it.

People who live away from congestion, pollution and the fear of earthquakes and floods must also have a better quality of life than those who suffer from these external costs. Organisations such as Greenpeace, who fight against pollution and other external costs, have an important influence on the quality of life for many people.

For a large number of people, discrimination greatly reduces the quality of their life. Ethnic minority groups and women in the UK have the law on their side and if the laws on equal opportunities are strictly enforced it should reduce discrimination and so improve the quality of life for many people.

The quality of life is a far wider concept than the standard of living, and it does not have a single measurement. An attempt to measure the quality of life would involve a number of factors. Some of these factors, such as peace of mind, cannot be measured.

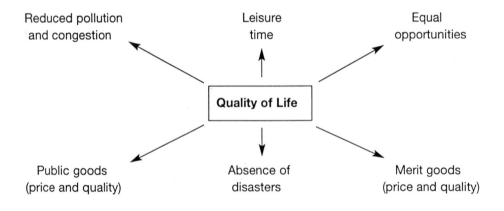

Figure 6.12 Factors Affecting the Quality of Life

Social Costs

We have seen that one of the costs of economic growth is an increase in social costs. Social costs, such as pollution and congestion, have an adverse effect on people's quality of life. However, economic growth increases output and provides more goods and services per person which increases the standard of living.

A very important conflict is therefore created. An increased standard of living should improve everyone's quality of life, but the process of increasing the standard of living actually harms people's quality of life.

Economic Prosperity

It is the function of an economy to produce as many goods and services as possible (economic prosperity). This should satisfy as many of the people's wants and needs as possible. However, people's wants and needs are never-ending, and an economy constantly needs to be increasing its output. If more goods and services are produced, GNP increases and GNP per capita also increases. Not only are more goods and services produced, but production creates higher income. This is a definite improvement in the standard of living.

Higher incomes, increases in goods and services and a better range of goods are more easily recognised by individuals than the social costs that may be created. As economies are run by governments who wish to be elected the greater output becomes more important than lower social costs.

■ Private wealth outweighs social costs.

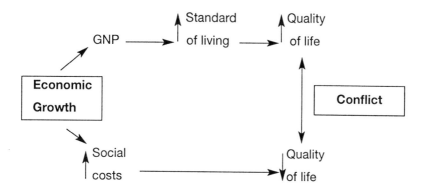

Figure 6.13 Economic Growth and Quality of Life

With the population in most countries increasing, due to a reduced death rate, the need for more goods and services becomes even greater. It is for this reason that economic prosperity is important. It also explains why the standard of living is often considered to be more important than the quality of life.

Review Terms

Standard of living; economic welfare; Gross National Product (GNP); GNP/load; GNP/per capira; inflation; quality of life; leisure time; merit goods; public goods; equal opportunities; economic prosperity.

6.5   Monetary and Fiscal Policy

The problems of unemployment, inflation and lack of economic growth are inherent in most economies. Their effects are so devastating upon the economy that when they occur the government must try to do something about them. They have a number of policy 'weapons' that they can use. These weapons, or policy instruments, can be divided into two groups: monetary measures (monetary policy) and fiscal measures (fiscal policy). Both monetary and fiscal policy are central elements of every government's economic policy.

Monetary Policy

Monetary policy is the control of the supply of money within the economy. It is put into action by the Treasury, acting through the Bank of England, on behalf of the government. An important part of the money supply has always been bank deposits and so any policy to control the money supply must be designed to control the commercial banks' ability to create credit. Thus monetary policy is a collection of methods designed to increase or decrease the number of bank deposits.

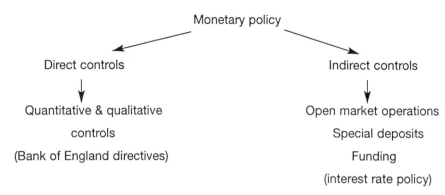

Figure 6.14 Monetary Policy

Direct Controls

Direct controls are either quantitative or qualitative controls. Quantitative controls would be a directive from the Bank of England on the amount that the commercial banks can lend, either as an annual or a monthly limit. This would also include strict credit limits and regulations on hire purchase terms. For example, the Bank of England could insist that the maximum loan for a new car was 60 per cent of its purchase price and the remainder could only be borrowed over two years.

Qualitative controls are again instructions from the Bank of England which tell the banks where they may lend the money. This can be to industry or consumers. It could be to exporters, importers, people buying UK goods or only to those investing in the purchase of capital. This would depend very much on what the government wanted to decrease or increase. These direct controls are instructions which the banks cannot ignore, they are controlled by the Bank of England and so must obey its orders.

Indirect Controls

Indirect controls are not instructions from the Bank of England but actions that they take which have an effect on how the commercial banks operate, thus it is an indirect influence rather than an order.

One indirect instrument is open market operations. This involves the Bank of England buying and selling government securities on the money market which affects the commercial banks reserves and their ability to create credit. If the Bank of England sells securities it reduces the commercial banks reserves and so decreases the money supply. If the Bank of England wishes to increase the money supply it buys government securities to increase the reserves of the commercial banks which increases their credit creation.

A further instrument is using special deposits. Each commercial bank is required to place with the Bank of England an amount of its deposits. The Bank of England has the power to demand that the commercial banks increase their deposits with them. These deposits become frozen assets, since they cannot be used by the commercial banks. This reduces the banks' ability to create credit and so decreases the money supply. An alternative is that the Bank of England reduces the special deposits that it holds and this increases the commercial banks' ability to create, credit increasing the money supply.

Funding is a further instrument available to the government. Funding is a process where the Bank of England replaces short-term treasury bills, which have a life of 91 days, with long-term government bonds. This reduces the commercial banks' liquid assets and their ability to create credit. Liquid assets can be quickly and easily converted into cash, and the more banks have the more loans they can make. If the supply of these liquid assets decreases then the banks have to decrease the amount of loans given, decreasing the money supply.

The rate of interest has always been the most popular indirect policy option. The government through the Bank of England was able to control the interest rate because of its position in the financial markets. If the Bank of England increased its own interest rate (the base rate) then the commercial banks and building societies followed. They may at some time need to borrow from the Bank of England and so cannot afford to have a lower interest rate. If the interest rate rises then less people can afford to borrow money and so less loans are made, decreasing the money supply. In 1987 the interest rate was removed from government influence. The Monetary Policy Committee (MPC) led by the governor of the Bank of England now decides upon the interest rate according to the market forces.

The rate of interest is the price of money, the cost of borrowing money. An increase in the price of money, the rate of interest, is the same as a decrease in the supply of money. The opposite is also true, a decrease in the price of money is the same as an increase in the supply of money.

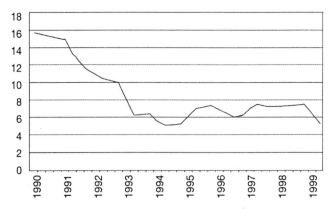

Figure 6.15 UK Base Rates 1990 - 99

(The Bank of England Rate)

All of the policies listed decrease, or increase, the supply of money within the economy. If less money exists then less goods and services can be produced, if more money exists then more goods and services can be purchased. Controlling the money supply therefore influences the amount of consumption and saving in the economy as well as the level of investment.

Fiscal Policy

Fiscal policy is made up of three weapons that are available to the government: taxation, government expenditure and Public Sector Borrowing Requirement (PSBR). The third element comes from the relationship between expenditure and taxation. If expenditure is greater than taxation then a PSBR exists. If taxation is greater than expenditure then a PSDR (public sector debt repayment) exists. Fiscal policy is a powerful set of weapons that are directly controlled by the government and they do not need a third party to put them into practice.

Government expenditure creates demand within the economy, therefore any change directly affects the state of the economy. Taxation alters the level of disposable income which affects the state of the economy. Both weapons have an effect on the economy by changing the level of demand that exists.

Government expenditure is usually on public goods and merit goods. Public goods such as defence and law and order are necessary for the economy. Merit goods such as education and health are vital for the well-being of the people therefore it is easy to increase government expenditure but very difficult to decrease it.

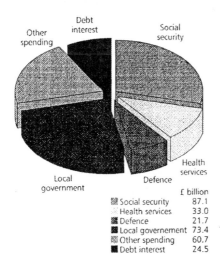

	£ billion
Social security	87.1
Health services	33.0
Defence	21.7
Local governement	73.4
Other spending	60.7
Debt interest	24.5

Figure 6.16 Government Expenditure

Taxation in the UK comes in many forms: income tax, VAT, excise duty, etc. It is a way of taking money away from households and firms in order for the government to provide the public and merit goods that are needed. This method is not very popular and so a decrease in taxation is very easy for the government. However, an increase in taxation causes many problems and is very difficult. It is also believed that changes in taxation have an effect on other factors such as workers' motivation.

Government expenditure is an injection into the circular flow and taxation is a withdrawal. The relationship between these two determines the size of the PSBR and PSDR. A PSBR is a budget deficit and a PSDR is a budget surplus. There are two schools of thought regarding the PSBR. Firstly it can be thought of as a transfer of wealth within the economy, borrowing that will be repaid when a budget surplus exists. The other view is that the PSBR actually increases the money supply within the economy and PSDR decreases the money supply. The Conservative Government (1979-97) tried to run a balanced budget, resulting in some years having a PSDR. The intention was that by reducing the growth of the money supply inflation would be greatly reduced, possibly even eliminated.

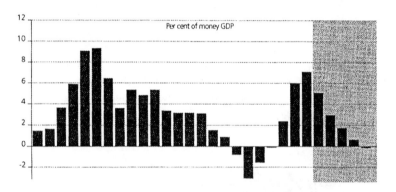

Figure 6.17 The PSBR in the UK

Specialist Cures

Apart from the traditional cures for inflation and unemployment a number of specialist cures exist. If the cause of inflation is rising costs, cost-push, then these costs must be controlled. Prices are difficult to control, but wages may be halted by using an incomes policy This stops wages rising above a set limit.

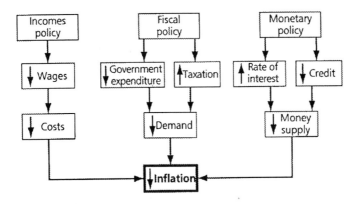

Figure 6.18   Incomes Policy

The specialist policy used to cure unemployment will depend upon the cause. Very little can be done to cure frictional or residual unemployment, and in a changing and developing economy a government would not wish to stop people changing jobs.

If unemployment is structural or technological then again the government can do very little to stop it and would not necessarily want to. In this situation the government would want to help the unemployed to find new jobs in new areas. This would involve retraining schemes and encouraging new firms to site in areas of high unemployment.

If it is believed that a natural rate of unemployment exists then the government will not attempt to decrease unemployment below this level. The policies used would be to decrease the voluntary level of unemployment by using supply-side policies. Any policy used would help the markets to solve the problem naturally. Examples would be to decrease benefits and income tax. This would encourage those who do not wish to work to find employment.

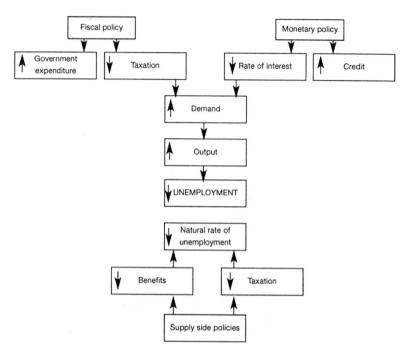

Figure 6.19

Review Terms

Monetary policy; fiscal policy; direct controls; indirect controls; quantitative and qualitative controls; open market operations; special deposits; funding; interest rate policy; government expenditure; taxation; PSBR; PSDR; public goods; merit goods; budget deficit; budget surplus; balanced budget; incomes policy; natural rate of unemployment; supply-side policies.

Reflective Pause

Government and the Business Environment

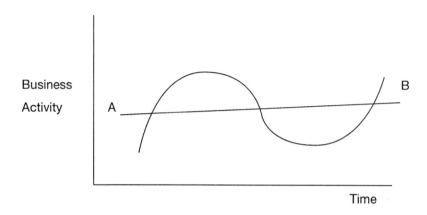

The previous diagram represents the various stages of the trade cycle. The line A-B shows the ideal increase in business activity which governments try to achieve.

Mark on the diagram the points at which the government might be expected to :

1. increase the standard rate of VAT;

2. improve hire purchase restrictions;

3. reduce Corporation Tax;

4. sell securities on the open market;

5. reduce interest rates;

6. reduce income tax;

7. impose special deposits;

8. increase public expenditure;

9. allow an increase in the budget deficit;

10 relax credit controls.

Be prepared to explain the reasons for your choices.

How appropriate do you consider these timings to be?

chapter seven

International Trade

The conditions and framework within which trade takes place between countries

7.1 The Gains from Trade

7.2 Exchange Rates

7.3 The Balance of Payments

7.4 The Problems of Trade

7.5 Government and International Trade

This section should enable students to understand:

- the importance of trade and the role of currency exchange
- the structure of the balance of payments account
- the problems that trade creates
- how governments can influence trade

7.1 The Gains from Trade

International trade helps countries to obtain goods and services that they cannot produce themselves; it also builds a strong friendship between the countries trading. The spread of technology is facilitated as countries trade. This is especially helpful to the less developed countries.

Climate is very varied around the world and so different countries can produce a range of products that other nations cannot. For example, in the UK we can produce wheat and potatoes but not oranges or bananas; in Spain the opposite is true. A major reason for the existence of trade is that countries are able to obtain the resources they need. Some countries have very few natural resources such as coal and oil while other countries have plenty of one resource. For instance, Kuwait has oil, but very little else. In this case, trade benefits everyone.

The workers in different countries have different skills, which may be the result of influences or of necessity. Some countries can therefore produce certain goods better than others.

The greatest benefit of trade is that countries are able to purchase goods and services that they would normally not be able to produce. This gives a greater quantity and variety of goods and services to the people of every country and increases their standard of living.

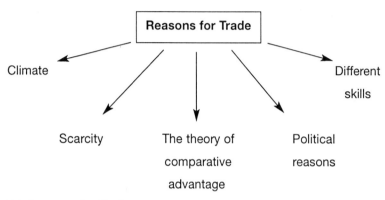

Figure 7.1 Reasons for Trade

The explanation for international trade is the theory of comparative advantage. This theory, produced by David Ricardo, emphasises the benefits to be gained through specialisation and trade. If countries specialise then they may gain from economies of scale and should produce goods of a higher quality at a lower price. Everyone should then benefit from a greater variety of goods at a cheaper price and of a better quality than if each country produced its own goods and services. David Ricardo's theory states that: If countries specialise in the production of that good or service in which they have a comparative advantage (can produce most efficiently) then after trading every country will be better off.

This means that countries should not produce for all of their needs but should specialise and trade instead. The theory, in simple terms, is saying that:

- first, countries decide which good or service they are most efficient at producing
- secondly, they should specialise in that good or service and maximise output
- thirdly, each country should trade freely, at a fair rate of exchange.

To show how the theory works in simple terms, assume that only two countries exist, both producing the same two goods. Both have the same quality and quantity of resources and factors of production. Money and transport costs are ignored.

	Cars		Wheat
USA	4,000	or	24,000 tonnes
Japan	5,000	or	20,000 tonnes

Table 7.1 Production Possibilities for Two Countries

In figure 7.1 the USA can produce either 4,000 cars or 24,000 tonnes of wheat but not both. Japan can produce 5,000 cars or 20,000 tonnes of wheat in the same time period, but again cannot produce both. These figures are their production possibilities which would produce a production possibility frontier.

If they decide to ignore Ricardo's theory and produce on their own they would have to devote half of their resources to each product and would therefore only produce half of the quantities shown in figure 7.1.

	Cars		Wheat
USA	2,000	and	12,000 tonnes
Japan	2,500	and	10,000 tonnes
World Total	4,500	and	22,000 tonnes

Table 7.2 Production without Specialisation

In figure 7.2 both countries have decided to produce both goods, ignoring the theory of comparative advantage, producing a world output for cars of 4,500 and world output for wheat of 22,000 tonnes. If the theory of comparative advantage actually works then both countries specialising and trading should increase the world output for both products.

The first decision to be made is, in which product should each country specialise. This will be an opportunity costs; the cost of producing cars, in terms of wheat that cannot be produced, and the cost of producing wheat, in terms of cars that cannot be produced.

USA can produce	1unit of cars or	6 units of wheat
Japan can produce	1unit of cars or	4 units of wheat
Step two		
USA	$\frac{1}{6}$ of a car :	6t of wheat
Japan	$\frac{1}{4}$ of a car :	4t of wheat

Table 7.3 Domestic Ratios and Opportunity Costs

Step one in Figure 7.3 is to take the lowest figure, the number of cars produced, and divide this into the higher figure, the amount of wheat produced. This produces a ratio: for every car produced in the USA six tonnes of wheat could be produced. In Japan for every one car produced four tonnes of wheat could be produced.

If this is put into opportunity costs then in the USA one car costs six tonnes of wheat and one tonne of wheat cost one sixth of a car. In Japan one car cost four tonnes of wheat and one tonne of wheat costs a quarter of a car.

In Japan a car only costs four tonnes of wheat but in the USA it costs six tonnes of wheat. Therefore cars are cheaper to produce in Japan that the USA. Japan is more efficient at producing cars: it has a comparative advantage in the production of cars. In the USA one tonne of wheat costs one sixth of a car and in Japan a quarter of a car. Wheat is cheaper to produce in the US than in Japan. The USA is more efficient at producing wheat than Japan: it has a comparative advantage in the production of wheat.

	Cars		Wheat
USA	0	+	24,000 tonnes
Japan	5,000	+	0
World Total	5,000	+	24,000 tonnes
	(+500)		(+2,000)

Table 7.4 Production after Specialisation

The lowest opportunity cost shows which goods countries should specialise in. The USA should produce cars.

The effect of specialising, shown in figure 7.4 is that Japan can produce 5,000 cars and the USA can produce 24,000 tonnes of wheat. If this is compared to figure 7.2 when the two countries produced both goods, it can be seen that world output has increased by 500 cars and 2,000 tonnes of wheat.

If this extra output is traded freely and fairly between the two countries then both nations will enjoy more cars and wheat than if they had produced both goods themselves. This proves that the theory of comparative advantage actually works: specialisation and trade benefits everyone.

Absolute Advantage

The example given in Figure 7.1 shows quite clearly that the USA is able to produce more wheat than Japan, and that Japan is able to produce more cars than the USA. It is easy to see where they should specialise and it is no surprise that the theory of comparative advantage actually works in this situation.

Ricardo claimed that his theory worked in all situations. If one country could produce more of both goods, it is said to have an absolute advantage. Ricardo believed that even in this situation both countries would benefit by specialising in that good in which they had a comparative advantage, and then trading freely and fairly.

	Cars		Wheat
UK	4,000	or	12,000 tonnes
Germany	5,000	or	20,000 tonnes

Table 7.5 Production Possibilities

In Figure 7.5 Germany is clearly better at producing both goods; it can produce more cars or more wheat than the UK. But even in this situation both countries can benefit by specialising and trading. Using the same process as before the domestic ratios have to be worked out and then the opportunity cost of each good can be found in each country.

Figure 7.6 shows the opportunity costs: it can be seen that car production is cheaper in the UK (three tonnes of wheat) and so the UK has a comparative advantage in the production of wheat. Wheat production is cheaper in Germany (a quarter of a car) than in the UK (a third of a car), so Germany has a comparative advantage in the production of wheat. Therefore the UK should produce cars and Germany should produce wheat.

UK

- 1 car = 3 tonnes of wheat
- 1 tonne of wheat = 1/3 of a car

Germany

- 1 car = 4 tonnes of wheat
- 1 tonne of wheat 1/4 of a car

Figure 7.6 Opportunity Cost Ratios

Figure 7.7 shows a comparison between world output before specialisation and after specialisation. It is necessary in this case for Germany to specialise in part but it proves that the theory of comparative advantage actually works, even when one country has an absolute advantage in the production of both goods.

Remember the theory of comparative advantage states that :

- if countries specialise in the production of that good or service in which they have a comparative advantage (can produce most efficiently) then after trading every country will be better off.

	Cars		Wheat
Before specialism			
UK	2,000	+	6,000 tonnes
Germany	2,500	+	10,000 tonnes
World Trade	4,500	+	16,000 tonnes
After specialism			
UK	4,000	+	0
Germany	700	+	17,200 tonnes
World Travel	4,700	+	17,200 tonnes

Table 7.7 Production Considering Specialism

7.2   Currency Exchange

When the UK trades internationally it buys goods and services from abroad and sells its own goods and services to other countries. The foreign countries need some form of payment for their goods and services and so does the UK.

Barter

One way to pay for goods and services from foreign countries is to use a barter system. The UK could exchange wheat for bananas and oranges, or oil for Japanese televisions. The problem with a barter system is that it needs a 'double coincidence of wants'. For example, if the Japanese wish to sell televisions, the UK must have the market for them. If the Japanese want some wheat but the UK does not want to exchange it, then the deal will not go ahead.

A further problem with barter is establishing the value of each good or service. How many tonnes of wheat equal one television, or how many gallons of oil equal one television, or one car? What if the oil or wheat is of poor quality? There are so many problems with barter that it is virtually impossible to trade using this system, and so an alternative has had to be found.

Currency

An alternative to barter is to pay for the goods and services purchased with money. The UK could buy Japanese televisions and pay for them with pounds sterling (£) and the Japanese could buy North Sea oil with Japanese yen. The problem with this is that the Japanese television manufacturers could not spend pounds in Japan and the North Sea oil producers could not spend yen in the UK.

What is required is for each country to be paid in its own currency. When the UK exports goods, such as oil, it should receive its payment in pounds sterling, and when it imports goods, such as Japanese televisions, it must pay for them in the currency of the country from which the goods are purchased; in this example it would be yen. If this system is to work there must be a way in which currencies can be exchanged.

The Foreign Exchange Market is a market in which all the currencies of all the trading nations of the world can be bought and sold. Any currency that is needed to purchase goods and services from another country can be exchanged for the home currency.

Exchange Rates

If currencies are bought and sold in a market situation then exchange rates need to be established. How many pounds equal one deutschmark (DM)?

The exchange rate is a price, the price of a currency in terms of other currencies. This price is just like the price of a commodity but in this case it is the price of a currency.

■ The exchange rate is the price of one currency in terms of the value of other currencies.

Price is established in the foreign exchange market in the same way that any price is established in any other market, by the forces of demand and supply. The demand for a currency and the supply of that same currency determine its price.

The reason for the demand for a country's currency is usually the desire to buy goods and services from that country, its exports. The supply of a country's currency exists because it is buying the exports of other countries (importing).

If the UK purchased cars from Germany, it would demand deutschmarks and supply pounds to the market in exchange. If France purchased oil from the UK it would demand pounds and supply French francs (FF) in exchange. Thus:

■ demand for a currency = the level of a country's exports

■ supply of a currency = the level of a country's imports.

There are other factors that may affect the demand and supply of a currency such as speculation and the flow of hot money which is deposited in whichever country has the highest interest rate.

Types of Exchange Rate

There are a number of different ways in which the exchange rate of a currency can be determined but these are all variations on two basic types of exchange rate, the fixed exchange rate and the flexible exchange rate.

The fixed exchange rate system is one where the rates are not determined by the market forces but where governments set the rate. The floating exchange rate system is totally the opposite; here the rate is determined entirely by the forces of demand and supply, without interference by government.

Fixed Exchange Rate

If a fixed exchange rate system is used the price (exchange rate of the currency) is set and guaranteed not to change. This rate, known as the par value, is known to everyone. For example: £1 = $1.50 and £1 = 2DM.

If for some reason the market forces did try to move the pound away from these fixed rates the UK government would intervene.

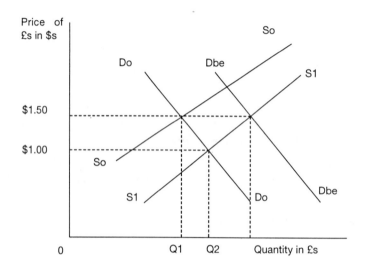

Figure 7.8 Government Intervention in the Foreign Exchange Market

In figure 7.8 the pound has a fixed value of £1 = $1.50 where DoDo = SoSo. If the level of imports increases the supply of currency will also increase to S1S1. The new equilibrium is at DoDo = S1S1 and the value of the pound should fall to £1 = $1, but because this is a fixed exchange rate it is not allowed to do so.

In this situation the Bank of England would step in and buy up the excess supply of pounds with its reserves of foreign currency. This would increase the demand for pounds (DbeDbe) and return the exchange rate to its previous value.

If the opposite occurred and an excess demand for pounds existed, the Bank of England would sell pounds and buy foreign currency to maintain the rate. This is government intervention.

The major advantage of a fixed exchange rate is stability. Every country knows the rate of exchange and unless a disaster occurs it will remain at this rate. The biggest disadvantage of this system is that it is expensive and it is difficult to keep the currency at the agreed value.

Floating Exchange Rate

A floating or free exchange rate means that the exchange rate of any currency is determined totally by the forces of demand and supply, the market forces. The rate can change daily or even hourly. There is no guaranteed value.

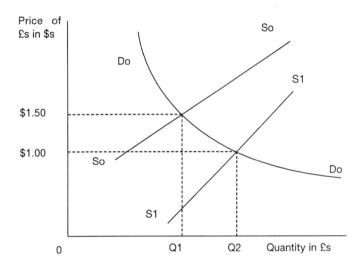

Figure 7.10 The Floating Exchange Rate

In figure 7.10 the original equilibrium is at DoDo=SoSo and £1 = $1.50. Imports have increased and are now greater than exports, therefore the demand for £s is less than the supply of £s. Supply has moved from SoSo to S1S1.

With a floating exchange rate the government does not intervene and the rate will fall from £1 = $1.50 to £1 = $1. This will make UK exports cheaper and imports into the UK more expensive. The big advantage of a floating exchange rate is that it is automatic, therefore it is easy and cheap to operate. This disadvantage is that it creates uncertainty in the world markets and harms international trade.

Other exchange rates systems exist, such as the exchange rate mechanism (ERM), used by the European Union countries, but these are variations of the two systems already explained.

Exchange Rate Problems

Exchange rates cause more problems for countries, and international trade generally, than any other factor. Should the exchange rate be fixed or floating? Is it the correct rate? How can speculation be stopped? These are just a few of the questions that have to be answered. Whatever the problems of exchange rates it is a fact that international trade would hardly exist without them.

Review Terms

Barter: pounds sterling; Japanese yen; foreign exchange; exchange rate; price; speculating; hot money; fixed exchange rate; floating exchange rate; par value; government intervention; exchange rate mechanism.

7.3　The Balance of Payments

When a country trades internationally it buys goods and services from other countries (imports) and sells its goods and services to foreign countries (exports). A country's exports provide it with income and its imports create expenditure. Like any individual, a country cannot spend more than it earns in the long run. In the short run if expenditure is greater than income a country may use its reserves, a country's savings, but eventually these will run out. A country may also borrow from other countries of the International Monetary Fund (IMF). However, if these loans are not repaid eventually no more money will be loaned out. It is for this reason that a country must make sure that over a long period of time its expenditure is not greater that is income.

Balance of Payments Account

If the levels of income and expenditure (exports and imports) are important then they need to be watched carefully. The best way to do this is to record all exports and imports. This record is called the balance of payments account:

■ a record of all external transactions between a country and the rest of the world.

The balance of payments account is split into two sections, the current account and the account that deals with transactions in UK assets and liabilities, often referred to as the capital account. The UK current account records the money value of every good or service exported out of the UK or imported into the UK.

	Exports (goods sold abroad)
minus	Imports (goods purchased from abroad)
equals	Balance of trade (visible balance)
plus	Invisible exports (services sold abroad)
minus	Invisible imports (services purchased from abroad)
equals	Current account balance (balance of payments on current account)

Table 7.11 The Structure of the Balance of Payments or Current Account

The current account is splint into two sections, the visible balance and the invisible balance. The total for goods imported is subtracted from the total for the goods exported and this gives the visible balance, or the balance of trade. Services and other transactions are recorded separately and, again, imports are subtracted from exports, giving the invisible balance. The visible and invisible balances are added together to give the current account balance, the balance of payments on current account.

Visible Trade

Visible trade is the export and import of goods that can be seen and touched, one of the easiest parts of the balance of payments to measure. All goods entering and leaving the UK need documents and so are easily recorded.

The export and import of goods are recorded separately to provide the balance of trade. This is important for the UK because it identifies any changes in the goods sold or purchased by the UK. This can in turn show changes in world markets, a lack of competitiveness by the UK or changes in world tastes and demand. As the UK has traditionally been a major manufacturer in the world these changes can be very important indicators of trading trends. Visible goods are classified into six main divisions for both exports and imports, with a seventh to cover any goods not recorded in the main six.

Category	In millions of pounds		
	Exports	Imports	Total
Food, beverage and tobacco	11,099	16,193	-5,094
Basic materials	2,754	6,279	-3,525
Oil	10,248	5,596	4,652
Other minerals	776	1,146	-370
Semi-manufactured goods	44,512	45,434	-922
Finished manufactured goods	100,466	107,182	-6,716
Other commodities and transactions	1,943	1,760	183
Total			-11,792

Source: The Pink Book, HMSO

Figure 7.12 UK Visible Trade - 1997

Invisible Trade

Invisible trade is split into three broad groups: services; interest, profits and dividends (IPD); and transfers. These are termed 'invisible' because unlike goods there is no visible product. The measurement of invisible is far more difficult than visible. There is no common point of measurement, such as a port or airport, and documents are not required in the same way that they are for goods.

The service group within the invisible category is split into five distinct services: government, sea transport, civil aviation, travel and financial services. IPD is split between the government and the private sector. This records earnings from overseas assets and the profits from subsidiaries of UK companies. Payments to overseas citizens for the same reasons are also included.

Transfers are also split between the government and the private sector. This includes items such as the government's payment to the European Union budget and gifts by UK citizens to friends and relations overseas.

Current Account

The UK's current account has constantly swung between deficit and surplus, with more deficits than surpluses. Traditionally the invisible account has always been in surplus and the visible balance has usually been in deficit, except when oil production was at its highest. The state of the current account often depends upon whether the invisible surplus is greater or less than the visible deficit.

Services	£m
General Government	-725
Transport	-2,405
Financial/Insurance	+9,060
Travel	- 3,597
Other services	+8,827
Interest, Profits and Dividends	
General Government	83
Private sector	12,085
Transfers	
General Government	1,287
Private sector	-4,817
Invisible balance =	£ 19,798

Source: The Pink Book, HMSO

Table 7.13 The UK Invisible Account - 1997

Transactions in UK Assets and Liabilities

The complete balance of payments account includes transactions in assets and liabilities as well as the current account. Whilst the current account deals exclusively with the sale and purchase of goods and services the transactions account shows money changing hands for assets such as machinery and factories.

This account also shows how any deficits or surpluses on the current account are dealt with. If money is taken from the reserves to pay for a deficit then this is recorded in the transactions account. The same would be true if money was added to the reserves, loans repaid or money borrowed. Investment overseas by UK firms, and payments owed to foreign firms, are also placed in this account; the purchase of stocks and shares is included as well as physical assets.

Figures for the transactions account are very difficult to collect because they come from a number of different places; some are inaccurate. This means that mistakes will be made. The problem is solved by using a balancing item. The current account plus the transactions in UK assets and liabilities account should produce a total of zero: they should balance. If they do not then errors have been made. The balance is achieved by adding the balancing item.

Items	£m
Current account	8,006
Transactions in UK assets and liabilities	-7,850
Balance (which should be zero)	+156
Therefore the balancing item	-156

Figure 7.14 The Balancing Item - 1997

The example in figure 7.14 shows an error of £156m. The current and transactions accounts should equal zero. An adjustment of -£156m is needed to achieve the balance: this is the balancing item.

The Complete Balance of Payments Account

The full balance of payments account will always equal zero: it is designed to balance, like a company's balance sheet. The importance of the account is that it records all the movements of goods, services, capital and paper assets for a country over a period of one year.

Items	£m
Exports	171,798
Imports	183,590
A Visible balance	-11,792
B Invisible balance	19,798
C Current balance (A+B)	8,006
D Transactions in UK assets and liabilities	-7,850
E Balancing items (C-D)	-156

Source: The Pink Book HMSO

Figure 7.15 The Complete Balance of Payments Account - 1997

7.4   The Problems of Trade

The balance of payments account, explained in detail in section 7.3 shows the income and expenditure of a country in its dealing with the rest of the world. A country, just like an individual, cannot afford to spend more than it earns. If this happens in the short run then the country may use up its reserves, its savings; it may even borrow from other countries or the International Monetary Fund (IMF). However, a country cannot do this for ever. Just as with an individual, loans have to be rapid. If a country continues to spend more than it earns; other countries and the IMF may refuse to lend to them, and eventually their savings, reserves, will disappear. It is because of this situation that countries keep a strict check on their balance of payments account and deal immediately with any problems that arise.

Balance of Payments Problems

If a country's expenditure is greater than its income then there is a basic problem with the balance of payments account. Income is earned from the sale of exports and expenditure is on the purchase of imports. The problem therefore is that imports are greater than exports. The country cannot afford to pay for the goods and services that it wants or needs to purchase.

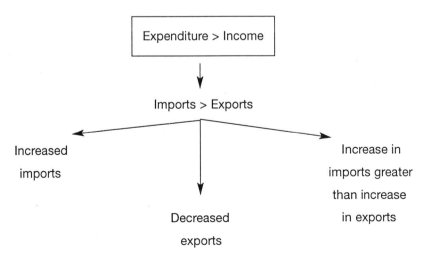

Figure 7.16 Trade Problems

The balance of payments problem is due to one of three causes:

- imports are increasing
- exports are decreasing
- imports are increasing faster than exports (exports are decreasing faster than imports).

Increasing Imports

There are many reasons why imports into a country may be increasing. If the income of a country is increasing then people will buy more goods and services and some of these goods and services will be imported. When income increases people are more inclined to purchase luxury goods. If these luxury items, such as television, videos and personal computers, are imported then the overall level of imports will increase.

It could be the case that the imported goods are not produced in the home country. If people gain a taste for these goods, or if they become fashionable, then demand will increase. A good example is the many exotic fruits that can now be purchased throughout the year in the UK. Previously these were only available in selected shops at certain times of the year. Consumers have become used to the variety and demand has increased. These imported fruits have increased in quantity, increasing the level of imports.

It is sometimes the case that goods from other countries have a reputation for reliability, or are thought to be of better quality than home-produced goods. A classic example is electrical goods. Japanese goods are thought to be the best. This reputation can be reinforced by prestigious brand names such as JVC, Sony and Panasonic. These factors increase the level of imports.

Foreign goods may be cheaper than home-produced goods. This could be due to inflation in the home country, more efficient production by the foreign producer or due to the exchange rate. Whatever the reason, if the foreign good is cheaper then the demand will be transferred to the imported good and the quantity demanded will increase.

Finally, if industry uses imported raw materials and increases its output as it expands, imports will also increase. Therefore, a healthy, growing economy will encourage an increase in imports.

Decreasing Exports

Some of the reasons for increasing imports can also be used to explain why a country's exports might decrease. If incomes within foreign countries decrease, due to unemployment for example, then their demand for other countries' exports will decrease. A general decline in the economies of overseas countries will mean that their industries will decline and the country's demand for raw materials will decrease, creating a decrease in the exports for the home country.

A country may get a bad reputation, as the UK did in the 1970s, for poor quality goods and failing to meet delivery dates. If this happens then the demand for that country's exports will decrease. A country's exports may become expensive due to inefficient production, inflation or a change in the exchange rate. Once again exports will decrease.

Less-developed countries tend to export natural resources, and as technology improves artificial substitutes are often produced. These substitutes are usually cheaper and more convenient to obtain and so the demand for the natural resources decreases, decreasing many LDCs exports. Finally it is a fact that natural resources are limited in supply and as they begin to run out the country concerned has less to export. This has been the case with the UK and North Sea oil: as the reserves have decreased the UK's exports of oil have also decreased.

Changing Exports and Imports

It rarely happens that only the level of a country's exports change (or the level of its imports). It is more likely that both will change at the same time. For example, exports could be increasing but imports could be increasing at a faster rate. Alternatively, both could be decreasing with imports at a slower rate. Both of these situations would cause a balance of payments problem for a country.

In these situations, several of the factors already discussed could be happening at the same time. For example, incomes could be increasing in the home country at a faster rate than the rest of the world, thus imports would increase at a faster rate than exports. Another situation might be that inflation in the home country was greater than in other trading countries, leading to a greater fall in exports than any decrease in imports.

Some Solutions

If a country has a balance of payments problem then it needs to do one of two things:

- increase exports
- decrease imports.

The ideal solution would be to achieve both of these at the same time. Increasing exports is a very difficult thing to do. A country cannot force other countries to buy its products and services, they can only encourage other nations to do so. This can be done by promoting a country's goods through trade fairs, producing the goods that everyone wants at a reasonable price, and trying to improve a country's reputation for reliability and quality.

Decreasing imports is relatively easier than increasing exports. Import barriers could be used but these invite retaliation which could start a trade war, with every country suffering. Import controls are also against the whole idea of the World Trade Organisation (WTO) and the European Union (EU).

A further policy is deflation. Deflation means that total demand within an economy is decreased. This decreases the demand for home-produced goods and imports. The economy is deflated by using fiscal policy, increasing direct taxes and/or decreasing government expenditure, and monetary policy, increasing the rate of interest to decrease demand. Deflation avoids retaliation but is less direct than import controls. The problem with deflation is that home demand is decreased which creates unemployment and bankruptcies for home producers.

A final policy option is to change the exchange rate of a country's currency. With a fixed exchange rate this would need a devaluation, but with a floating exchange rate a depreciation of the currency would be needed. A devaluation or depreciation is a decrease in the value of the currency. For example, if £1 = $2 then a depreciation/devaluation would change the exchange rate to £1 = $1.

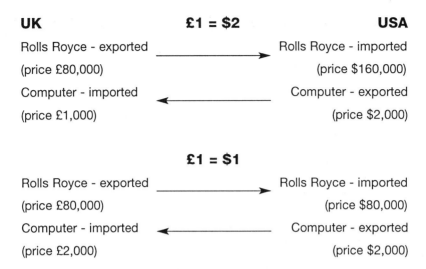

UK   **£1 = $2**   **USA**

Rolls Royce - exported   Rolls Royce - imported
(price £80,000)   (price $160,000)
Computer - imported   Computer - exported
(price £1,000)   (price $2,000)

£1 = $1

Rolls Royce - exported   Rolls Royce - imported
(price £80,000)   (price $80,000)
Computer - imported   Computer - exported
(price £2,000)   (price $2,000)

Figure 7.17 The Effect of Exchange Rates on Prices

The effect of depreciation/devaluation is clearly shown in figure 7.17. After the depreciation/devaluation the price of the Rolls Royce exported from the UK to the USA decreased from $160,000 to $80,000 in the USA. At the same time the import from the USA, a computer, increased in price in the UK: it was £1,000 and increased to £2,000.

The total effect of a devaluation/depreciation is that the price of exports decreases and the price of imports increases. This should decrease the demand for imports and increase the demand for exports, correcting the balance of payments

---

Review Terms

Exports; imports; income; reputation; exchange rate; trade fairs; trade war; import barriers; General Agreement on Tariffs and Trade; European Union; deflation; fixed exchange rate; devaluation; floating; exchange rate; depreciation.

7.5   Government and International Trade

If the balance of payments gives a government cause for concern, then it is possible to act in order to remedy a problem.

Variations in Exchange Rate

If there is a fixed exchange rate in operation, then a devaluation of the currency will make exports cheaper and imports dearer, and so will help to remedy the situation. If there is a free or fluctuating exchange rate, it should be dealt with by market forces. If this is not the case, then the government can instruct its central bank to sell its own currency on the foreign exchange market. This will increase the supply of the currency available for sale, and thus will lower the price, and so have an devaluing effect.

There are other techniques available to any government to remedy balance of payments problems. These include :

- Tariffs, which are taxes on imports. They increase the price of the good in the country, and also provide the government with a source of revenue. They can be used on specific products or to limit the imports from particular countries.

- Quotas, which are quantitative restrictions on imports. These, again, can be used to exclude specific goods or the produce of particular countries. They can be applied rapidly, if speed is of an essence.

- Inter-government request. One government can ask another to ensure that it limits its exports, with the underlying threat that firmer action could be taken if the request is ignored.

- Exchange controls. These can be very effective, as the government determines who has access to foreign currency. As anyone wishing to purchase foreign goods is normally expected to pay in a foreign currency, to prevent individuals and firms from owning foreign exchange will seriously hinder imports into the country.

- Physical controls Most countries ban the import of particular goods, such as weapons and drugs. This list can be expanded, to suit the policy needs of the government.

The arguments for import controls are varied, but can be split into several sections - economic, and political and social.

Economic Arguments

To Protect Infant Industries

All countries are at different stages of economic development, so one nation may have a well-established industry which is merely beginning to emerge in another. Many would consider this as a threat and the newly-established industry would not survive the competition of a more mature rival. The argument is that such fledgling industry should be protected from competition until it has become more mature. In many ways, this depends on political attitude. Those who are dedicated to the notion of competition would reject the argument, while others would maintain that, without some form of protection, new industries would not be able to emerge.

To Enable Industries to Decline Gradually

The argument here is very similar. An industry may decline in one country, but prosper in another. To prevent the worst aspects of the structural unemployment that results from the decline, it is possible to protect the industry, so that it declines more slowly, and thus allows redeployment of the workforce.

To Eliminate Dumping

Dumping occurs when goods are sold in a foreign market cheaper that in its domestic market. This can destroy competition, and put the exporter in a monopoly position, to the clear detriment of the domestic economy and consumer.

To Correct a Temporary Balance of Payments Deficit

If the deficit is anything other than temporary, then other measures would be needed.

To Protect Industry

Firms often complain that they are unable to cope with 'unfair' competition, such as goods made by 'sweated labour', and thus they ask for protection. All arguments of this type have three difficulties:

- they deny comparative costs
- they may provoke retaliation
- they begin the international trade cycle.

Retaliation

If one country imposes import controls, then the recipient is likely to retaliate. The danger is that such behaviour would bring about further retaliation, and eventually lead to a trade war.

To Help Reduce Domestic Unemployment

Again, this can cause serious repercussions :

- retaliation
- the international trade cycle.

Political and Social Arguments

To Preserve Areas in Decline

A region may be suffering from decline and so, in order to prevent the disintegration of the region by some of the inhabitants moving away to find alternative employment elsewhere, the government may protect the industries, and thus preserve the jobs. This is most likely in rural areas, where the population is relatively sparse in the first place.

To Promote Political Policies

If a government is in dispute with another country, then it can intervene in international trade to pursue its foreign policy. For example, the USA has, for many years, banned trade with Cuba because it disapproves of the regime in that country. In the same way, Britain has often refused to allow trade in armaments with countries whose policies it dislikes.

Of course, this is a contentious issue, as such principles reduce trade, and thus cause unemployment. Needless to say, some other country will not be involved in the dispute and will supply any requirements, so the government invoking the ban is not succeeding in preventing the actual acquisition of goods.

The question is of morals against economics. Should you trade with a country whose policies are, to you, immoral, even if this costs your citizens money? There is no answer to such a question, and each individual will have an opinion.

To Promote Political Ties

Before Britain joined the European Union, it had a trade policy which encouraged trade with the countries which were part of the British Commonwealth. This had the additional effect of making these nations more friendly to Britain, and also politically closer. By joining the European Union, such trading ties had to disappear and, instead, Britain became closer in trading relations with the other members of the

European Union. Any form of trading agreement must bring participating countries closer.

Review Terms

Devaluation; tariffs; quotas; exchange controls; physical controls; infant industries; dumping; retaliation.

Conclusion

In the pursuit of a greater variety of goods and services and ultimately a better standard of living, countries have continually increased their trade with one another. Whilst the gains from trade, as outlined by the theory of comparative advantage, are obvious. The problems are numerous. With such a diversity of laws, monies and cultures, problems are inevitable.

It is to the area of international cooperation that the Western industrialised nations are increasingly devoting their attention. The meeting of the G7 and the development of trading blocs such as the EU are evidence of this. Unfortunately in the course of this development many of the poorer nations in the world who need to trade to survive are often being forgotten. It might be said that international trade is a rich countries club.

Reflective Pause

Buy British

Margaret Charrington is the Director of Invest in Britain. She believes that if every household spent £10 a month more on British-made goods, the national trade deficit would be reduced by £6.5 billion a year, and many more jobs would be created. However, it is not always easy to find British-made goods in the high street shops. In 1993, members of Townswoman's Guilds asked chain stores about this. Here are some replies:

Woolworth

'We would like to have more British products if Britain had a better marketing policy and more competitive goods ... We stock the best value for money, nine times out of ten it is not British'.

Dixons

'Only 5 per cent of our stock is British'.

Marks and Spencer

'For modern fashions, we have to go abroad to find quality and innovative ideas'.

Even Mrs Charrington regrets that 'our cutlery designs were slow to adapt during the 1980, and goods continued to be made that could not be used in dishwashers or microwaves. She was sad 'to see how little ... money is being spent on design'.

Source: adapted from the *Daily Telegraph* 6 August 1993.

How to Encourage Local Industry

Fergal Quinn owns a chain of supermarkets in Ireland. They are called the Superquinn chain. He has decided that all Irish-made goods will be highlighted on the bills of shoppers. 'If only a fraction of business switches to Irish goods, we would create lots of jobs very quickly' he said.

The Irish government has been trying to persuade Irish manufacturers to indicate clearly that goods are made in Ireland, but the 'Buy Irish' campaign only met with limited success. Feargal Quinn's decision might revive it.

Areas for Consideration

1, How would the highlighting of Irish-made goods and 'Buy Irish' markings help the Irish economy and its balance of payments?

2. What are the potential problems of the 'Buy Irish' campaign?

3. Margaret Charrington has suggested that the solution to the British

balance of payments problem is for every family to spend £10 a month

more on British-made goods. Would this be effective?

chapter eight

The Problems of Government Economic Policy

The conflicting nature of a government's economic aims

8.1 Internal Conflicts

8.2 International Influences

This section should enable students to

- understand the aims of government
- understand the conflicting nature of policy objectives
- understand the international influences on a government's policy objectives
- question the benefits of greater international collaboration and interdependence

8.1 Internal Conflicts

All politicians expressed similar concerns and made similar promises. It would be inconceivable to hear a politician announce that unemployment was unimportant and, if elected, that his or her party would do nothing about it. In the same way, everyone seeking election cares passionately about the level of inflation, and would seek to reduce it to a low level. Economic growth would give greater prosperity to all and, therefore, is a certain election pledge. All of this would be assisted by ensuring policies to restore our international trading position by tackling any balance of payments deficit.

Such statements are not unique to British politics. They are features of parties throughout the world. Just as the bar room pundit can select an English or Scottish football team that would win the World Cup, an English cricket team that would win all of its test matches or, on current performances, a Welsh or Irish rugby team that would devastate the opposition, so the politician makes pronouncements about how much better everyone's lives would become if their party attained power.

It would be useful to examine the validity of such promises. The problems of, for example, unemployment, are clear. In economic terms, anyone who is unemployed is a wasted resource. Moreover, not only are the skills of the unemployed not being used to benefit the economy as a whole, in addition there is a cost to the state of unemployment pay and other benefits. Revenue that is used for such payments could either be used to provide improved goods and services to the community at large, or could result in reductions in taxation which would give everyone greater spending power. There is also a social cost to unemployment. There is a high level of personal indignity, which can lead to depression, which in turn damages the quality of family life. Higher rates of depression, suicide, violence and other crime can result from this. Of course politicians wish to reduce unemployment. Who would not?

Inflation is clearly another problem. If Britain's unemployment rates are higher than elsewhere, then British goods and services are rising in price in relation to those of countries with lower inflation rates. Thus, British goods and services will grow in price when compared to those of our foreign rivals. This means that foreigners will be discouraged from buying British while, in Britain, foreign goods and services will appear increasingly attractive. As a result, fewer British goods and services will be purchased, resulting in less income, less prosperity, and greater unemployment. Clearly, therefore, inflation needs to be controlled and it is the responsibility of politicians to devise policies to effect this control.

If a country suffers from a regular balance of payments deficit, that means money is regularly leaving the country to pay for the debts incurred. As the wealth departs from a country, so it becomes poorer and poorer, and thus less and less able to pay its debts. Eventually, it will no longer be able to finance its deficit, so exporting countries will suffer from the onset of the international trade cycle, and the country itself will be left to survive on its own modest resources, providing that it has not already sold those resources to help pay the deficit. No country wants to be in such a position, so any sensible politician must be prepared to tackle the balance of payments problems.

Each successive generation expects to be more prosperous than its predecessor. Standards of living measured in material terms do seem to rise rapidly, although not all of the population recognise this. For example, in the 1950s, few people possessed televisions but, by the 1970s, most households could boast of a black and white set. At the start of that decade, colour sets were rare, but by the middle of the 1980s most people owned colour televisions. At that time, ownership of video cassette recorders was restricted to a small proportion of the nation but, today, most families have at least one. Such examples of improvements in the ownership of material goods could be duplicated with a wide variety of products. The soldier returning from the Second World War may have dreamed of owning a car, but settled for a bicycle or, perhaps, a motorbike, whereas today most households own a car. Yet there is a constant demand for improved standards of living, and regular accusations that they are falling. No politician would ever think of announcing that this is irrelevant. To be elected, candidates need to be able to create an image of a future so bright that the electorate wishes for that future. This means that there must be economic growth, for it is assumed that greater prosperity will result, and this will be shared by the nation as a whole by way of a general improvement in the standard of living.

Thus, politicians are likely to promise that they would like to achieve, simultaneously, low unemployment and low inflation, combined with high levels of economic growth and balance of payments equilibrium, or even surplus. Such promises are easy but, in truth, far less easy to achieve. Let us examine each of these issues.

Unemployment

It would be fairly easy to reduce unemployment. This could be done, for example, by creating a budget deficit and reducing taxation. This would mean that take-home pay would increase. Households with more money to spend would buy more goods and, as long as those goods are British, this would mean that more goods would have to be produced, so more people would have to be employed. Those people, formerly unemployed, would now have more income, and so would buy more goods, etc., and so the multiplier effect would take over and the unemployment would fall.

By ensuring that more goods are being made, and more people are employed, then economic growth would result. Unfortunately, the closer to full employment the economy goes, the more likely it is to suffer from inflation.

Inflation

All of the evidence from such sources as Professor Phillips and other economists, such as Professor Paish, point us to that conclusion. The other problem is that the more prosperous a nation becomes, both in terms of economic growth and high employment, then the more likely that country is to buy imported luxury goods, which, of course, would worsen the state of the balance of payments.

Balance of Payments

In other words, to achieve low unemployment and economic growth is reasonably easy, but at a cost of growing inflation and balance of payments difficulties. If a different approach was adopted, and the initial policies were directed towards control of inflation, then this could be achieved by ensuring that demand within the economy was controlled. This could be done by reducing the amount of money available in households for expenditure. An increase in taxation would be suitable. Whenever personal spending falls, fewer and fewer imported goods are bought, so this would also be an effective control of the balance of payments.

Unfortunately, to reduce spending means that fewer goods will be bought. If fewer goods are bought, then fewer goods need to be made so that economic growth is decreased. Also it means that fewer people need to be employed, and so there is an increase in unemployment. Thus, this approach would control inflation and ensure that the balance of payments situation remained under control, but at the expense of falling economic growth and rising unemployment.

This suggests that it is not possible to achieve simultaneously the four major economic objectives. However, that really implies a rather negative analysis. True, it does appear that full employment, zero inflation, high economic growth and a balance of payments surplus may not be attainable, but such ambitions are excessive. What a government might hope to achieve is a balance of the four aims which satisfy the people.

In other words, effective economic policies can ensure that employment is at a level which satisfies the economic aims of the ruling party, while inflation is sufficiently low that no-one feels aggrieved. Such a balance between inflation and employment ought to produce a level of economic growth which allows increased prosperity, but not such a high level of growth and employment that excessive imports are encouraged.

The various political parties have established different priorities, and so will achieve different balances. For example, when Mrs Thatcher became Prime Minister, she maintained that the biggest threat to the British economy was inflation, and so she pursued policies intended to tackle inflation. This included use of interest rates and the result, as might have been expected, was an increase in unemployment. She accepted this, despite fierce criticism, as the price that had to be paid for her war on inflation, coupled with modest or even no economic growth.

The Labour Party, in opposition, denounced the evils of unemployment, and stated that, on achieving office, this would be their priority. This would have meant a higher rate of employment, balanced by higher inflation, higher economic growth and, in all probability, deteriorating balance of payments figures.

Whatever the balance, if the government has worked to achieve it and the people are prepared to accept it, then the government will not lose popularity. However, beware of the politician who promises to provide all of these objectives.

Speculation, through the changes it creates in the value of a country's currency, can create inflationary pressures or unemployment. A major financial crisis in the Far East can lead to the heavy purchase of the £ sterling and its increased value; harming export industries as well import substitution industries.

All of these factors have ignored the influence each event would have upon the economic growth rate of the country and its balance of payments. This would complicate the situation even further.

8.2 International Influences

The problems faced by all governments in the pursuit of their economic aims is further complicated by the influences from other countries, an international influence that has in the past 40 years increased markedly.

In the last 40 years the improved modes of transport, and the enhanced transport infrastructure on an international scale, has vastly increased and improved the links between all countries. The transport factor, coupled with enormous advancements in technology, has brought about a rapid growth in international trade and a reliance of countries upon one another. The obvious benefits of such progress, a greater range of products and cheaper goods, has at times been outweighed by the problems that have been created. The term of global economy is commonly used and interdependence of countries actually creates a situation not unlike that of a single economy.

Within the UK the aim of the government might be to keep the level of unemployment as low as possibly and maintain stable prices. However, within the European Union (EU) it could be that the level of unemployment is very high. This would result in a decrease in the demand within the EU for UK goods. Consequently the demand for UK exports would decrease and those industries would need to reduce output and make workers redundant, resulting in increased unemployment. Traditional policies such as fiscal policy would not help to solve this problem. This would be a classic case of outside influences affecting the aims of the UK government.

A further example, and a common one, is that of inherited inflation. A country such as the UK relies heavily upon imported raw materials. If inflation exists in the country from which the goods are being imported then the price of the imports will rise. If no alternative exists this will force up the price of the good produced in the UK, unless the producer can make cost savings elsewhere. These increased prices are the start of the cost-push inflationary spiral. If the goods produced are for home consumption and export, the increased prices will decrease the levels of exports and create unemployment at the same time. It should not be supposed that solutions to these problems do not exist but as outlined previously these solutions can have conflicting results.

The UK Government of the late 1980s was often criticised as a one-policy administration. If unemployment has been caused by unemployment elsewhere there is a need to make goods purchased from the UK even cheaper. This can be achieved by decreasing the value of the £ sterling. To do this it may be necessary to decrease the rate of interest. The effect is to create extra demand in the UK and so possibly fuel inflation whilst also making imports more expensive and definitely applying inflationary pressure.

The reverse situation of increasing interest rates to combat inflation will appreciate the value of the £ sterling. This in turn makes exports more expensive and imports cheaper so decreasing the demand for exports and at the same time reducing the demand for those home-produced goods that are in competition with imported goods. Once again unemployment results.

One result of the improvement in technology has been the growth in the international finance markets. Shares and currencies are traded daily on the various markets and, due to the large sums involved, are open to speculation of all kinds. The consequence of this advancement in technology is often that a currency may 'move', depreciate or appreciate, due to the actions of others.

Speculation, through the changes it creates in the value of a countries currency, can create inflationary pressures or unemployment. A major financial crisis in the Far East can lead to the heavy purchase of the £ sterling and its increased value harming export industries as well import substitution industries.

All of these factors have ignored the influence each event would have upon the economic growth rate of the country and its balance of payments, which would complicate the situation even further.

The government's pursuit of any economic objective is extremely complex. The need to balance each of the factors whilst taking into account issues on a world-wide scale, and trying to predict events globally, makes any policy decisions and target setting so complicated that the question must be asked: are the benefits of closer links with other countries not outweighed by the problems?

A solution could be the integration of the member states of the EU and the use of a single currency, or would this just reduce the problems? There is no simple answer to such an intricate situation, which is further complicated by the political views of those who make the decisions. In fact it could be said that this is possibly the most difficult problem to overcome: to separate the economics from the politics.

Reflective Pause

Representatives from the country of Barengo are paying a one week visit to the Treasury here in London.

Here for Help

They are trying to gain some knowledge of the help an economy can receive from the collection and interpretation of statistical information - the economic indicators that are so familiar to us.

Inaccurate Data

Barengo does not have a problem with unemployment at the moment, and it is careful to ensure that the balance of payments is in equilibrium. There is economic growth, but the measurement of its rate may not be accurate.

There may be inflation, but again, the figures are not necessarily correct. The officials are aware of the major aims of economic policy, and they are seeking to develop systems of record keeping that will ensure their data is accurate and up-to-date.

Assessment

The ways in which other indicators can be used to assess the performance of the economy, and to flag potential problems in advance, really interest the Barengans; their presence here in the UK demonstrates their desire to maintain an improving economy.

Areas for Consideration

Write a report to assist the visitors. In it you should consider the following :

1.   What is the value of economic indicators?

2.   Explain why governments find it difficult to achieve all four simultaneously?

3.   Why is inflation a major danger to any economy, but particularly to a developing country such as Barengo?

accelerator 102-4

balance of payments 136 *et seq*, 153-5
    assets and liabilities 139-40
    invisible trade 138
    visible trade 137-8
Bank of England 68-9, 118-20
break-even analysis 22-3
British industry 38-42

Confederation of British Industry (CBI)
    66
costs and revenues 19-23
    break-even analysis 22-3
    costs 19
    profit 19-22
    revenue 19
currency exchange 132-6
    barter 132
    currency 132
    exchange rates 133-6

decision making Ch 5 *passim*
    civil service 90
    financial institutions 91-2
    formal 84-5
    media 92-4
    other influences 86 *et seq*
    public opinion 94-5
    spin doctors 90-1

economic growth 111-4

    advantages 111-2
    costs 113-4, 117
    problems 112-3
    prosperity 117-8
    quality of life 115-6
    standard of living 114-5
economic institutions Ch3 *passim*
economic problem Ch1 *passim*
    circular flow of income 24-30
    solutions 30-5
economic systems 30-5
    market economy 33-4
    mixed economy 34-5
    planned 31-3
    traditional 31
economies of scale 46-8, 51
employers' associations 66
European Union 80-2

Factors of production 3
financial institutions 66-70
Bank of England 68-9
    banks 67
    building societies 67-8
    insurance companies 68
    stock exchange 70
fiscal policy 118-24
flow of income 24-30
    basic economic problem 24
    injections and withdrawals 29-30,
    26-7
    open economy 28

three sector economy 27-8

two sector economy 24-6

governmental framework Ch4 *passim*

    central 74-5

    local 75-6

    taxation 76-9

government economic policy Ch8 *passim*

    internal conflicts 151-5

    international influences 155-6

industry, development/growth Ch2 *passim*

    British 38-42

    internal organisation 52-7

    size/location 42-52

    specialisation/exchange 42-5

inflation 104-11, 153

    cause 105

    cost push 108-9

    demand pull 105 *et seq*

    in Britain 110-11

International Monetary Fund (IMF) 81

International trade Ch 7 *passim*

    balance of payments 136-41

    currency exchange 132-6

    gains from 126-32

    government and 146-9

    problems 141-3

    solutions 144-5

less developed countries (LDCs) 1, 42, 143

market forces Ch1 *passim*

Marx, Karl 30

monetary policy 118-21

    direct control 119

    indirect control 119-20

    multiplier 101-2

organisational structure 52-7

    charts 54-5

    span of control 55-6

    types of 59-62

price mechanism 7-8

    demand 7-12

    market, the 15-8

    supply 12-5

private sector 61-2

production 4-7

    choice 4-5

    distribution 7

    how to produce 6

    opportunity cost 5-6

profit 19-22

    maximum 21-2

    per unit 19-21

public sector 59-60

public sector borrowing requirements (PSBR) 121-2

revenues 19 *et seq*

scarcity Ch1 *passim*

    factors of production 3

    wants and needs 1-2

Smith, Adam 30-1, 44

specialisation/exchange 42-5

taxation 76-9

trade cycle 100-1

trade unions 63-6, 70

unemployment 98-104, 153

    accelerator 102-4

    causes 99-100

    multiplier 101-2

    trade cycle 10-11

wants and needs 1-2

World Bank 82